THE SAVIOUR OF THE WORLD

VOL. III

THE KINGDOM OF HEAVEN

By

Charlotte M. Mason

Public Domain
Charlotte M. Mason
Original Publication Date: 1909

This book is Part Three in a multi-volume set
of poetry covering the life of Christ.

Reprinted 2015

Simple Pleasures Press
Auburn, Washington USA

Minor alterations have been made to the content by the current Publisher. The painting reproductions in the original were left out. The original text did not have subheadings—the descriptions used in the Index were added to each section to serve as titles/sub-headings for clarity while reading.

ISBN-13: 978-1514752999
ISBN-10: 1514752999

THE SAVIOUR OF THE WORLD

VOL. III

THE KINGDOM OF HEAVEN

CONTENTS

PREFACE - 7

OVERVIEW OF VOLUMES 1 & 2 - 15

BOOK 1

OF TAKING THE KINGDOM - 21

BOOK 2

PARABLES OF THE KINGDOM - 53

BOOK 3

ADMINISTRATION AND THE KINGDOM - 103

BOOK 4

THE BEGINNING OF THE HOLY WAR - 125

INDEX - 173

"He that unto God's kingdom comes
Must enter by His door."
                    RICHARD BAXTER

PREFACE

(Critic and Author: a Dialogue)

Cr. Forgive my dulness that I fail to see
The work's intention; —if a single plot
On the vast sphere of thought and fact it stakes,
Hedges about, bring under ordered tilth.
Is it a Life of Christ? A hundred men
Have writ in whole or part the Life of lives:
All are rejected, falling short as they must
Of that surpassing fitness marks the *Four*.
Au. E'en so falls to the lot of every man
To restate for himself, on his own plan,
That which we name the Gospel: not his Creed—
Restatement there shall curious vapours breed! —
Far other work is his, as line by line,
His mind absorbs the history divine,
Figures each scene, weighs well each pregnant word
Let fall in sequence due by the Good Lord
Who came, our WISDOM, down to teach mankind
The WAY, the END, the way marks each shall find
For every step of the road. Wise men of Greece,
Those Easter sages, too, taught, —Man's increase
In wisdom for the ordering of his days—
His righteous first pursuit and all his praise:
He came not to destroy what these had taught;
But rather to enforce that Wisdom, wrought
But ways and words of God in mind of men:
No easy lesson this; once and again,
"Now; have ye understood?" the TEACHER cries: —
And we, so slow of heart to realise
That there is aught a child may not perceive,
Or more than fool is able to believe!
High sounding teaching our vain minds demand,
Nor know at all—we do not understand!

Cr. I see: you would unfold what might be named
Christian Philosophy if full-proclaimed;
Your heifer, friend, has been in many a plough!

Au. You hit my purpose partly, I avow;
but the *Method* of the Master seems to me
Too subtle-wise for any man to see
But who hath deeply pondered in his heart;
For see, Christ's teaching is no separate part,
A sermon here, there a miracle, event—
Or Birth in Bethlehem, or how He went
Afoot through all their hamlets doing good,
Healing all sickness, giving men their food;
And all in casual wise, occasion-moved:
There is, I take it, tho' scarce fully proved
The fact, yet evidence the Saviour meant,
Say, single sheet by sheet, to unfold His intent
As men should show capacity to meet
his thought with thought reciprocal; we know
No words of teaching any further go
Than the measure of his mind who hears that word:
This limitation to His work, our Lord
Accepts all graciously, and lays His plan
To catch the ear, mind, heart of every man,
Arrested to attention by some sign
In this mechanic-world of life divine.
So all His works, as pictures, illustrate
Utt'rances mystic, opening mysteries great;
And every teaching fits with all the rest;
And all's profound, progressive, asks our best—
The eager student's utmost labouring zeal
To comprehend, to know, to inly feel: —
Thus, diligent, He teaches; now, by law,
By fable now, or miracle, will draw
Men to consider. Ever one theme
His teaching labours; Word and Work 'twould seem
Are used t'elaborate some truth divine

Till, lo, at last, His hidden meanings shine
Revealed to men, no more to be obscured,
Although the disciples only are assured.
That lesson taught, another cognate theme
The Lord pursues with patient skill supreme.
Till that be comprehended, if by few—
The Twelve, perchance; through months doth He pursue
With many variants—sayings, acts and ways,
A single theme, shall fructify our days:
Thus, in the months this volume would include,
Teaching about THE KINGDOM is pursued
By our dear Lord, through miracle and tale,
Example cited, what may best avail
To win men's thoughts from emulous greed and strife
To that must be sole business of their life!

Cr. I see your point of view; men would attend
Schools of the sages, days, months, years on end, —
Their sole concern to master, thought by thought,
Philosophy with aids to living fraught;
this you demand for Christ?
    Au.   Aye, this and more;
For who as He God's image can restore?

Cr. But you forget the temper of our days;
Never had Christ more lavish generous praise;
That He, the ideal Man, not one denies;
Starlike, serene, doth still His image rise
Above the troubled waters: but, see you,
The line of argument you must pursue
Demands a certitude we don't possess:
The Son of Man we're ready to confess—
Not we, Confessors in the ancient sense
Imperill'd life and limb! —yet are we sure,
his loveliness must long as time endure:
but all His several words, those wonders, signs—
The Critic, look you, is abroad; divines
Here, textual error by a method sure;

There, chronicle will not the tests endure
Science applies to that she can receive:
Now, face the matter squarely; how believe
The "Gospel truth" our wisest hold in doubt?
Nay, that we clear the Christ from all the rout
Of controversial issues is our praise!
 Au. But what a Christ is He on whom your gaze
With sentimental rapture fix ye! See,
Those Pharisees, more logical than ye!
"Blasphemest thou!" they cry when He employs
Attributes of the Almighty: a man enjoys
Twofold, deny, still voluble in praise!
Trifling inaccuracies—these but prove
Men wrote those things that they had learnt to love
Hear four men tell what happened in the street
This very day, —how do their tales compete
For credence? Not because they are agreed,
But, this man tells the tale with better heed
To what is possible! Now, here we fail;
Just here our usual methods won't avail!
Nothing is "probable" where HE is concerned;
Our art of reasoning must be all unlearned:
Suppose, Dimension Fourth, that ancient quest,
Sudden disclosed itself to seeker blest; —
What errors would men make! How hard to wrest
Their thought from the old measures, length and height
And ponderosity, —confined them quite,
Set bounds to speculation! It is plain,
That new conditions, measures, must obtain;
The new Dimension, —its own standard, test;
All things thenceforth are meted at behest
Of the new basic fundamental laws
Inherent in that absolute new-found cause!
Changes so vast in measures, values, all
That constitutes the worth of life, befal
The man who sees THE LORD; know Him, indeed,

The single MEASURE which shall not mislead
That man would try the truth, for TRUTH is He,
sole standard of the truth needs must He be;
To try His words and acts by any rule
Obtains without Himself, is as if fool
Should measure miles in quart-pots, yards in scales!
"Behold, I make a new thing!" What avails
Each petty test, pedantic, when the vast
Of Personality Divine goes past
Our dazzled eyes? No other help is brought; —
We must *see Christ* ere poor scale of our thought
Apply to his dimensions, infinite,
The VERY GOD amongst us! We may write
The breadth and length of miracle and word,
Then only, when we measure by the Lord

   Cr. I see; you reverse the usual way;
First, know the Unknown; that learned, why, thought may play
About the records, measuring them by trained
Conception of their Subject; —how obtained?

   Au. Straight plunge we in dimension all unknown!
"New Birth," the Master calls it, who alone
Could speak of that He knew.

   Cr.   And by what sign
Shall one discern in himself this life divine?

   Au. To answer were to say in single word
All, in three crowded years the disciples heard
From the lips of the Master.

   Cr.   This, disclose;
How may a man be certain that he knows?

   Au. Perhaps, by this; a new dimension straight
Reveals itself in him; he walks elate,
Enlarged, unlimited; with passions, powers,
For which no scope he found in th' slow dull hours
Of all his former life! Constraining love,
A pent-up passion, shall his doings move:

A tremulous lover goes he, quick to grieve
O'er wrong he does to love; apt to believe
And linger tenderly o'er every word,
Precious as pearl, hath fallen from his Lord:
Ambition, power and place? All these the man
Finds in his master's service; petty span
Of personal issues, projects, holds him not; —
In joy of THE KINGDOM all himself's forgot!
And see what scope is his—the round world, all,
Shall at his Master's footstool one day fall;
And his to advance that End, by tool or pen, —
Or aught brings solacement or strength to men!

   Cr. The allurement of such prospect, I confess;
Of life for his living, every man goes less;
He prods him with the spur of this and that
Desire, ambition, —soon, he ambles flat;
Like stranded fish, he gasps for fuller life
Than comes with children, power, or wealth, or wife:
I own our need; but doubt is in the air:
Has so-called Higher Criticism no share
In furthering the issue all desire?

   Au. Is it not, too, of God? The purging fire
Shall fine the Word itself; but surer, He,
Than record of the word; by Him, we see
If any saying be indeed divine, —
So shall His glory through the letter shine!

   Cr. Allowing for the argument's sake your view,
Still your first allegation must be true,
Each man must ponder for himself to *know*.
Then what is gained, when into verse you throw
The tale we own inimitable; word,
The like of which by men hath not been heard?

   Au. Never rude Crucifix by roadside set
But doth, in some poor heart, new thoughts beget
Of Jesus, Lover of mankind and Lord!
May it not be that every sincere word,

Rough-carven, poor unworthy though it be,
is not without appeal to them who see
That here is one in simpleness would show
That fragment of the truth 'tis his to know?
And look you, thought breeds thought; whoever thinks
And drops his thought in word, where that word sinks,
New thought springs up, created by impact
Of thought on mind laid open; to react
In ampler juster thought; increase we thus
To measure that Stature set for us!

CONTENTS OF VOLUME I

THE HOLY INFANCY

*ANGELS and prophets long had searched in vain
Those mysteries, now, for wayfarers writ plain:*

*How Christ was born in Bethlehem of pure Maid,
How to three kings His Rising was displayed:*

*How holy Simeon blessed Him and foretold
His Mother's grief, He, sacrificed and sold.*

*How out of Egypt did God call His Son
That all the prophets figured might be done.*

*How, simple Child, He dwelt in Galilee
That simple folk His light might daily see.*

*How to Jerusalem in His twelfth year
He went, before Jehovah to appear:*

*How there He shed His light, a duteous Boy,
To keep the law His errand, not destroy.*

*How eighteen years of meek submission then
Prepared Him for His labours amongst men.*

*How He went out to John to be baptised,
And John in Him a greater recognised.*

*How in the wilderness for Forty Days
He bare assaults of Satan. Give we praise!*

How in Cana He made the water wine,
That men should see of life in Him a sign.

How in Jerusalem quick drave He forth
The traders and their wares—of how small worth!

How journeying north to Galilee once more,
He sate and taught that Woman heavenly lore.

How all the men came out who heard His fame,
And, SAVIOUR OF THE WORLD, did Him proclaim.

These things have we considered as we might,
And hence would meekly follow in His light.

CONTENTS OF VOLUME II

HIS DOMINION

CHRIST healed the rich man's son: the man believed;
"God is a spirit," the lesson he received.

He preaches to His own; mad hate they bring, —
Would from sleep brow of hill the Saviour fling!

People who sat in darkness saw great light
Whose brightness baffled unaccustomed sight:

Those fishers four on Sea of Galilee
The fishers of the Lord were called to be:

At Capernaum Christ preached: the people heard,
And knew Authority was in His word.

Vile spirit bade He forth in that same hour,
And all men recognised an unknown Power.

Peter's wife's mother, raised from fevered bed—
By hand that raised her would thenceforth be led.

"At even ere the sun was set," they came
To Him for healing, sick and blind and lame.

Then wearied, He, a great while before day,
Went out to desert place that He might pray.

The folk of Galilee would make Him King;
He knows how little worth the praise they bring.

Weary with preaching, Christ bade put to sea; —
Behold, a wondrous draught, the fishers' fee!

A leper cried, Thou canst, —wilt make me clean?
I will, saith Christ; healed, who had leprous been!

Levi took customs' dues by the seaside,
And when the Master called, he straight replied.

His Jews rejected for hypocrisy;
Too skilled in subterfuge, what hope have we?

Man at Bethesda's pool so long had lain—
The Lord who healed him to betray was fain!

Christ taught, —the Father and the Son were One
In words They spake, in all works They had done.

On the Son the royal crown of judgement set; —
He learned the ways of men, nor would forget:

In Him was Life; and all the souls that live
Draw breath from Him, to Him their praises give.

The Law, the prophets, witness; to each heart,
The Father testifies, and shows his part.

Thy Jews condemned, grant us, good Lord, to heed—
Unstable in our faith, slack in our deed!

Christ walked in cornfield on the Sabbath day,
And set men free from bondage whilst they pray.

He instantly the withered hand restores,
And, grieved, the Rulers' faithlessness deplores.

Once more to fair Genesareth He came,
And multitudes drew nigh, with love aflame.

Our Founder chose the Twelve, and laid them, sure
Stones to sustain that Church which shall endure.

He charged them; told them, how the poor are blest;
How persecutions should their lives molest;

Taught them the brother-secret; how to give;
How with all men as brothers they should live.

Of blind man led by blind man, cupboard's store,
Of building House of Faith, He told them more:

And then He climbed the Mount that all might hear, —
That multitude had come from far and near:

"Blessed are they that mourn," He told the sad; —
With promise of the Father's care made glad.

Chaste must they be and kind and guard their speech; —
For God's own holiness is in man's reach.

He taught men how to give their alms, to pray;
And all their anxious fears to put away.

Behold, the Church He founded on that day
Received those Institutes should guide her Way.

The people heard, and hardly understood,
But knew the Word He spake was very good;

Perceived Authority in every word
And fain would bear due fruit of that they'd heard.

BOOK I

OF TAKING THE KINGDOM

I

THE CENTURION'S SERVANT HEALED

SIX days the Father worked—and, lo, the world!
The Almighty rested on the Seventh day.
Work comparable for processes begun,
For magnitude of issues, deep design,
Had Christ the Son wrought on that blessed day
When He called forth His Church, and—it was good,
That new creation, now to have a name
And blessedest uses for the sons of men!

A man outworn with giving all he has,
Or wealth, or thought, or love, or what he has,
Falls emptied, as sky-vessel drained of air;
And, quick, new ministrants are set to work
To lift him, prostrate; with new hopes, inflate:
The Father of us all graced His own Son,
Begotten of Him ere the worlds were made,
E'en as He graces any o'er-spent soul;
But, for the Son had wrought a vaster thought
Into expression than a man might work,
There was conferred on Him more perfect gift,
And adequate, than comes to any man.
Christ sought once more the city of His choice;
There, waited Him the elders of the Jews
Who ruled in synagogue: a plea they brought
And earnestly they urged for sake of him,
The Gentile friend who loved them and had built
For them their synagogue: man of clear mind,
This Roman soldier, —captain stationed there,
In garrison at Capernaum, —not of those
Who let men's notions, practices, beliefs,
Pass him all unconcerned: he would fain know
What meaneth this or that, why do ye thus; —

Answer, heart-searching brought: God of the Jews,
Jehovah,—more than Caesar, than all gods:
All spirit forces His, to bid or chide;
All must subserve His will Who all has made:
Well, then, for him to honour this great God,
Almighty, with his substance, kindly care
For the Jews, His chosen people!
                                    Aware was he
Of things new-manifest in Capernaum;
Claim to authority, could any weigh
More certainly than he, who Caesar's right
Supported here in province far removed
But, Caesar,—his the power that comes of place,
Another Caesar should hold equal sway; —
This prophet of the Jews, supremacy
He wielded as a man swings his right arm
In labour of his choosing. Power of God
Was his, to do or to refrain; reveal,
Keep hid: did God indeed impart HIMSELF,
His sole authority? Or, was this—GOD?
That righteous man, of trained integrity,
Found much to ponder in the common talk
Of Jesus, filled the mouths of all the folk.

Calamity o'ertook this good man's house;
A servant whom he loved, —perhaps, who knows?
A foster-brother, with him from the breast,
And holding charge of all things for his lord, —
Lay in his house now at the point of death
And grievously tormented, palsy-struck:
Watching his servant's anguish, all his thoughts
Turned whither they had turned for many a day:
Authority was present in the world,
Could bid, not men alone, all ministers
Of health or sickness, happiness or grief, —
Authority supreme: but how approach

This uncrowned Potentate? A Roman, he
With what plea might he move this princely Jew?
Clothed with humility as good men be,
E'en when they sit controlling subject race,
This noble Roman sought his friends' good word;
And they, the Jewish elders, came to Christ
And praised their friend: "Worthy is he," they say,
"That Thou shouldst do this for him, for our sake!"
And, Jesus, "I will come and heal the man;"
And He went with them, ever prompt to hear
The prayer of friend for friend. Elate, the Jews
Went with Him in their midst right glad to serve
The man who them had served, nor arrogant
Had shown him to them, subject.
                                       He alone,
This Roman soldier, saw beyond the seeming,
Perceived immeasurable condescension
Of Him upon the road to his poor house!
Intolerable to him that One so great
Should serve his servant, take a step to please!
So, friends he sends to the approaching Christ; —
"Lord, trouble not thyself," their eager word
From him, "Not worthy I, that Thou shouldst come
Beneath my roof; not worthy thought myself
To come to Thee and pray my servant's life:
Why shouldst Thou come to heal? But speak the word,
And lo, my servant shall be well. I know
How one with servants bids and is obeyed;
I am a man under authority—
The thing which I am bidden, that I do;
And under me are soldiers; Go, I say,
To this one and he goeth; Come, to that,
And on the word, he comes: Do this, I bid
My servant and he does it. Lord, I know
How biddeth he who hath authority
And how his servants hasten at his hest;

Health is Thy servant, health and very life!
But bid them and they run at thy command!"

When Jesus heard these words He turned Him round,
Marvelling at greatness of the gift this man
Had laid at His feet: and to the multitude
Who followed, saith He, "Verily, I say,
No, not in Israel have I found such faith!"
Faith, great in comprehension! Many proofs
Of faith had Israel offered; see the Twelve,
How they left all and followed Him: how John
Knew Him the Lamb of God that taketh away
The sins of all the world; but here, a man,
Doth more than love, serve, follow to the end;
Doth more than see the Hope of Israel,
Fulfilment of all promise! What, say they,
What more is left for any to believe?
Giving his heart, what further can man do?
Yea, verily, there is a greater faith,
Begot not solely of a nation's hope
Fulfilled for loving hearts: this faith is much:
But, single-eyed intelligence to see
With seraph keenness, how, if God be all,
All things that come and go in human life
Must at His bidding come, go at His word:
To see, that if One speak the Word of God,
E'en to forgive men's sins, then, of a truth,
Not to another giveth God His power
And He who doth these things—the Son of God!
The faith to compass this is fit reward
Of that integrity which worthy thoughts
Concerning all things worthy entertains:
Such an one sees the truth, and seeing, loves,
Frankly embraces, and tenacious, holds!

"This Roman presageth a mighty host,
Men of just mind, thronging from east and west,
With faith like his: tho' not of the kingdom, they
With Abraham, his son, and his son's son
Shall sit in heavenly places; while true sons,
Woe worth the day! outcast shall find themselves,
In darkness, where is weeping and dismay,
Because they had not faith to know the hour
Of visitation by the Son of man!"
We may not let things pass, nor understand,
Nor ask ourselves if God be in the world,
Nor what He meaneth by the signs He sends:
Who scans his heart in this wise, he hath faith,
And, lo, to faith, the promises!
                            Meanwhile,
The Centurion, following his friends, drew nigh;
The Lord discerned him, spake the word he craved, —
"Thou, blessed, go thy way; as thou believ'dst,
So be it done to thee! Nor questioned he,
But found within his house—the sick man whole:
And more than life of friend gat he that day;
To faith was added love; he knew the Lord!

All faith is graced of God; there be degrees;
Their "great" and "little" faith men brought to Christ,
An offering in their hand, and all, He took;
But not with equal favour; how should men
Else know gift most acceptable to God?
According to his insight is man's faith;
In measure of his faith, he gives his love,
And ample service issues from great love.

II

"INCREASE OUR FAITH"—THE DISCIPLE

A CORD there is which heaven doth use to bind
Two lives in one; —with such considerate care
In fixing each to each, that thus they grow,
The two, one higher being: the strength of each
So strengthen'd is; the beauty, beautified;
While the thin places in each character,
Pieced and sustain'd by strong parts in the other,
Do safely so endure the wear of life.
Nor doth this hold for closest bond alone,
But for the casual commerce of an hour
'Twixt thee and any other by the way.

Of three bright differing strands this cord is spun:
Two, from a heavenly wheel, are straight run out;
While from his substance man the third doth fetch,
Just as some spider draws wherewith to make
Her web from her own body: yet is this
A heavenly product like the other twain,
But diff'ring from them, in that from the first
'Twas lodged in man's bosom; —or less or more,
According to the will that draws upon't.
This 'tis his part to take and wind with those
In triune strength invincible. Should he fail,
Or draw with niggard or uncertain hand,
The other two, still running out to seek
Full measure of this third wherewith to twine,
Knotted and tangled grow, and fret the lives
With many a let and hindrance they had else
Bound in fair symmetry and entire strength:
Knowledge and love and faith, —of these is spun
That threefold cord not to be broken soon.

No bidding of the will may summon love,
And not of duly noted acts and words
Comes the perception of another's being:
As little of ourselves are these, as moods
Of gloom and gladness born of changes wrought
In the quick face of nature.
                          Too much we think
To rule ourselves, the while our Author holds
Our spirits all responsive 'neath His touch,
And plays upon them with His winds and light
And subtle influences in the air,
And mystic sympathies with men and things, —
All in our eyes too light for passing thought—
Which yet do mould us into that we are.
But though our bliss or woe come not of us,
Receptive power is lodged in every breast;
All may reject or take, and this it is
That rules the differing pitch of human lives:
Think'st thou thy puny faith shall God exceed?
Or, niggard, canst believe enough in man?
Open thy being wide—it shall be filled;
Suspicious guard all inlets, —sadly prove
The aching famine of an unfed heart!
According to thy faith, the friend thou know'st,
According to thy faith, shall prove thy God!

III

THE RAISING OF THE WIDOW'S SON

A SORROWFUL procession filled the way
As Jesus came to Nain—with multitude,
Disciples and chance following; —those came
Adown the street to city gate, and sounds,
Mourning and lamentation, rose to God
To plead with Him for piteous woes of men,
Women left desolate with none to fend,
None tenderly to cherish. She, poor soul,
That widow in their midst, appealed to all,
Neighbors and kinsfolk, by her utter loss;
What was there left, her strong young son laid low
On bier they bore before her? Widow, she,
With none to get her bread and none to love!
So they all mourned with her, kindly folk,
Whose utmost was a cry to God:
But HE was very far; the youth was dead;
Would the great God do ought for a dead man
Should comfort weeping mother?

                              As they neared,
The mourners and their burden, city gate, —
Wherefrom the dead pass out to burial
In place remoter from the homes of men, —
Behold, another multitude drew near,
And, by the city gate, the two crowds met:
Pity was not so far from that sad soul,
The desolate Mother; God was not removed;
He had compassion on her; bade them stand,
Who bare the bier; and the poor mother bade,
"Weep not!" Strangely arrested, stayed her tears,
E'en as ours do when He bids cease to weep.
And, He, the LORD, drew nigh and touched the bier, —
(With touch, held hope, for who would lightly touch

The defiling dead?) In sudden awe they wait,
The breathless multitude, nor know for what,
But omen they perceived—portending, sure,
Awful event, cognition unconceived, —
Checked pulse, stopped breath, of all the waiting crowd!

Where, Death, thy victory? HE spake the word—
"Rise, young man, I say!"—And, lo, the ear,
Passed out of hearing of all mortal speech
To silence unimagined of the Dead,
Was not beyond recall of this one Voice:
"The Dead shall hear," He had said, and this dead man
Heard, and forthwith obeyed; arose and spake!
Mother and son forgot by folk who heard,
An instant awful thought struck them to heart—
Should they not die? Had they not all their Dead?
Lo, here is One who holds the keys of Death,
Unlocks the dreadful door and summons back
One gone forevermore from wonted ways!
And each one in his heart, —I too shall die;
Within hearing of His voice shall I remain?
Terror of Death was chased from every heart
At thought of human speech to reach him there,
In uncongenial kingdom of the Dead!
No more as yet, but what a hope were here!
Continuance, friendly offices, and help, —
If these, beyond the Grave, why fear to die?
With awe they gazed on Him who spake the word
That called the dead to Life: new hope was born,
And all their hope, embodied in that MAN
Whose tones immediate reached to those unknown,
"Remote, unfriended" regions of the Dead!
Nay, reached with words of Life! The dead can live,
And this MAN hath the keys of Life and Death!
One kingdom they, an easy way between;
And, if One rule the twain—why fear to die?

Thus Christ restored the widow's son to life
And dropped a seed should grow in many hearts
Though none brought faith or prayer to woo His deed:
The dead, can they have faith? Grief hath no room;
And all the crowd had pity, but not faith;
The Lord of His sweet bounty gave them that,
Conditions other gifts; now, had they faith.
What of the young man? He must follow, sure,
That Saviour who had called him from the dead?
Christ gave him to his mother: once again
She had a man from the Lord; at first, a babe,
And now this strong young son who wrought for her!
Was ever mother thankful like to this?
Was ever mother joyful like to this?
City of Nain had witness in its midst
Should yet proclaim the Name of Him who spake,
And, lo, the dead man rose and was alive!
He, the young man, what questionings of him;
What wonder and desire searched his heart, —
The Dead, did they in truth go on with life,
E'en as did he? And, dead and living both,
Had they one Master, able to command
Them, whither they should go, what they should do?

More than their own concerns of death and life,
The people thought upon the Lord, and feared:
"Behold," said they, "a prophet, in our midst
Has risen to us, unworthy, praised be God!"
All through Judaea the great news was spread
By tongues of those who saw and those who heard,
And all men knew, —God, come among His folk!

IV

JOHN BAPTIST A PRISONER

WHERE now is John—
Round whom in wilderness
The eager people press,
Confessing sins with tears
And overwhelming fears;
Who bade them put away
Their sin against the day,
That great day of the Lord
Of which he brought them word: —
"Repent, and be baptized,
Else, rotten, be excised
From the Branch!"
Now, where is John, who knew
Messias, in that Jew
Came to him at the pool, —
Would follow, meek, the rule
Good for all men, and prayed
Baptism of John, dismayed;
And he baptized the Lord
At His so gracious word! —
Where now is John who in a man
As other men, was graced to scan
Lineaments of the Lamb,
Sent by the great "I AM,"
Descended from His throne
The whole world to atone,
In sacrificial blood,
With the all-loving God!
Where, John, who bore that witness true
And fearless spake the truth he knew?

In desert still he dwelt;
But, bound, no longer felt
Winds of the waste blow free;
No more his eye might see
Least thing that moved at large
To far horizon's marge;
Shut in by fortress walls,
His soaring spirit falls;
He doubts and is dismayed; —
"By what then is delayed
The coming of our King
Who shall salvation bring?
Is He indeed the Coming One,
And I, here, languishing alone?"
Ah me, that Prophet's faith should fail
When doubt and dreariness assail!

V

THE MESSAGE OF JOHN

PRISONER in fortress by Dead Sea—
Whose waters all the living flee, —
The Baptist, Bedouin in heart,
Wilderness bred nor having part
With them who live shut in by walls,
(Abhorrent lot his soul appals),
Confined the Baptist lay; his past
O'er him its shifting shadows cast;
The shadows only came that day;
No past so bright, its light may play
Upon our hours of desolate gloom;
And John for hope could find no room,
Or joy, in all his retrospect!
Not now with gladness might reflect
On multitudes that came to hear,
And be baptized ere Christ appear!
Delusion was it, then, that call
He thought he answered, yielding all?
And that dear moment at the Pool,
He met Messias, —like a fool
Had he let hope, fallacious, blind
Him to the truth? Had his own mind
Fashioned the Christ he fain would find?
Disciples came to see him still,
Allowed of Herod, at their will;
These told him all the land was filled
With fame of Jesus; how He willed,
And, lo, all human ills were cured, —
The very dead to life restored!
Would he, their Master, bid them fly,
Proclaim that this was Christ in truth,

Or that delusion had in sooth
Possessed the people's heart? Behold,
How secret thoughts like flowers unfold,
And after their own kind make fruit!
What had the Baptist said should bruit
His faithless questionings forth to men?
But, let a thought prevail, and then,
Shouted from housetop, lo, the word
Scarce by thy secret soul was heard!
Now, see, occasion at his hand;
John sends the two with curt demand, —
Art Thou indeed Messias, sent,
Or for another look we?
                Spent
With all the speed they made, the two
(Had journeyed half the country through),
All travel-worn and breathless came
To where Christ was: the blind, the lame,
The sick, the sad, had gathered there,
Whose woeful state addressed a prayer
To Him, the Merciful; nor stayed
John's messengers, on whom was laid
Their master's urgent hest, till He
From doing good at leisure, be;
They cried with insistence rude,
"John Baptist sent us to Thee," (crude
In thought and rough in speech were they),
"His word, Art He that cometh, say,
Or for another do we wait?"
Their petulant speech Christ heard; and straight,
In that same hour He many healed
Of sin and sickness, plagues revealed
In eye of day; and then He spake; —
"Hence, to your master; with you take
True tale of that ye've seen and heard;
Lepers are cleansed; deaf, hear the word;

The blind receive their sight; the dead
Are raised to life; the poor man hears
Good news with unaccustomed ears:
Tell John these signs; he knows to read;
And add this word: —When occasions breed
Doubt and disloyalty to Me,
Who stumbleth not in darkness, he
Is blessed; and him I name My friend
Who trusts me constant to the end!"

The people heard word of reproof
To Baptist sent: for their behoof
Christ witnessed of His servant John; —
Like commendation, who hath won?

VI

The Lord Testifies of John

"What went ye out to wilderness to see?
Reed shaken with the wind? A man whose words
Sway this way, that way, lightly moved by breath
Of popular favor, will of priests or kings?
I tell you, nay: this man spoke only truth,
Nor swerved for any fear or any hope;
Nor spoke the facile word should please the crowd!"
Not unsubstantial reed, —a mighty tree,
The Baptist stood, to weather every blast;
His roots deep-seated, forehead raised aloft,
And arms outspread to shelter multitudes!

"But what then, to behold, did ye come forth?
Man in soft raiment clothed, whose easy days
Are delicately nurtured? Such as these
Dwell not in wilderness, but, in kings' courts,
Apparelled gorgeously, they sun themselves!
I tell you, nay; the man ye went to see
Was he whom no man owed, for all his need
The wilderness supplied; who took no heed, —
What shall I eat? what drink? where lie tonight?
Nor prized his life for any vain delight;
Whose strivings of the spirit kept him hid
In wilderness till God should come and bid.
For what indeed was't ye went out to see
A prophet of the Lord? yea, right were ye;
Ye knew by every sign a prophet, sent,
Witness to bear for God; the folk to chide
For their backsliding ways:
But John is more!
Prophets full many have to Israel cried;
But John is he of whom this word is writ, —

'Behold, My messenger before Thy face,
The way before thee to prepare, I send.'
The King discerned he, one among a crowd,
Nor thought him worthy to unloose the shoes
Of Him, the Coming One! His office, great,
For great of heart is he, for great work fit;
I tell you, I who know, that among men
Of woman born, no greater hath arisen
Than John the Baptist; see ye honour him!

"Greater than any born of woman is he,
But there be others, of the Spirit born;
Wherefore, for all his greatness, mark ye this, —
One little in the Kingdom is more than he!
What meaneth this? ye ask, What Kingdom, then?
God's Kingdom is in the heart of every man
Who yields undoubting fealty to the Son:
Outside are many righteous; none of these,
Greater than John the Baptist! But, see ye,
Not John himself could bear continual fret
Of things not understood, nor doubt at all!
Blessed the man who saith, 'Lo, I believe,
Groping in darkness, yet, do I believe!'
Nor suffereth any cloud to hide the KING.

"Ye think, to take the Kingdom, easy task;
That any Jew who knows Messias come
Is straightway in the Kingdom when it comes:
Look you, the Kingdom's not for any man,
Nor for the Jews, to see it when it comes;
The Kingdom is among you, nor see ye,
Because your eyes are sealed. The man who sees
Looks not for pomp of kings nor any state,
Nor frets him, as doth John, that shows of power
Befitting kings are tardy; seeing the King,
His eyes are lightened; scale of values new

Orders his thoughts: what was of highest worth,
E'en praise and gifts of kings, are to him nought;
And that he cared not for, nor knew it were,
Lo, that his sole desire and all his praise!
Shout of a King in midst of his hid life,
Rule of a King in all his quiet days,
Service of King at all hours calling him, —
A man in the Kingdom hath he room for more?

"Joy of the kingdom is exceeding great;
But never happy State but hath its foes,
Hind'ring who would come in. Kingdom of God
Is not for th' easy man: in other States,
The man would prosper labours day and night,
Pushes his cause, pleases, and serves and waits
On him who grace dispenseth, the crowned head!
The Kingdom of heaven suffereth violence
From days of John till now; who hath eyes to see,
He pusheth strenuous in; the violent man
Taketh his heaven by force! 'Wherein,' say ye
'Shall men use violence in this hidden life?
Nay, we are ready to take arms for Thee
And drive the Roman hence! What more wouldst have?'

"But I would have ye fight another war
With other foes at the gate—such foe as John,
Much honoured, well-beloved, hath quailed before!
Ye shall not doubt, though all men disbelieve,
Ye shall not fear, though earth's foundations shake, —
Ye, who are of the Kingdom! Keep ye faith
Though all the world beleaguer you with doubts
And terrors manifold; full violent be
To seize and hold in face of all assaults
The goods of the Kingdom ye have eyes to see!

"I tell you no new thing: the prophets all,
The Law ye hold by, witnessed until John,
These things I tell you; greater, he, than all!
Till John, the truth, an ever-gath'ring stream
Rolled with increasing volume down the years,
Each prophet adding that word told to him:
But John—he saw fulfilment! 'Lo,' he said,
'The Lamb of God that taketh all men's sins!'
Ye wait Elijah, as the prophet saith?
Will ye receive it? The word hath been fulfilled,
And John, the Elijah of expectancy!
He that hath ears to hear, now let him hear."

The people praised God who had given John—
Of whom were they baptized. Who have done well
Are ready to do better; glad, they heard
While Jesus spake of John; the Pharisees,
And they who taught the Law, would none of him;
That first rejection forced them still reject
Christ's word of the Kingdom violently attacked;
City should be beleaguered four-score years,
Should many hundred years be trenched about—
New generations coming to th' assault
With arms of its age; behooves, who keep,
Attack, defense, provision as they may;
But sit at ease? Not for a single day!
The violent keep the City; strong ones take;
The siege is without truce; Watchman, awake!

The Lord beheld the crowd and knew their mind:
With fickle malice, praise they John, to blame
Jesus the Christ; or praise Christ to defame
The ways of John: "To what then are they like,
Men of this age, whereunto shall I liken
Their moods unstable, their ill-ordered thoughts?
Like children are they in the market-place

Calling, each row to each, Ye will not play!
We piped to you, and, lo, ye would not dance!
We mourned to you, ye did not weep in turn!
(Good that He watched the children at their play,
Our Lord so tender-sweet with little ones:)
"So is your mind, ye men of Israel!
For John the Baptist came, eating no bread
(The common food of men), nor drinking wine;
A man whom none might blame for any grace
He did his flesh: ye say, a devil hath he!
The Son of man is come; He eats and drinks,
As all men eat and drink; no separate life,
But common life of men ye see Him live:
Behold, say ye, man, gluttonous, given to wine!
Nor pause to speak the truth or know the truth:
Fickle opinion sways you,—floating light
As thistledown o'er every gathered crowd,
Tending this way or that at breath of each!
'Then, Which is right,' say ye, 'hard life, denied
By a man's will of every common ease
That falls in his way as berries to the birds,
Or his, who like a bird, takes and goes on,
Nourished for flight and stirred to gracious song?'
Nay, both are right, nor any rule of life
Shall ease you of your labour of free choice!
Whatso a man doth well, that is well done;
Who walketh lowly with his God shall act
As his own heart doth move; for, justified
Is Wisdom of her children—this and that!"

VII

THE DISCIPLE DREAMS THAT HE SEEKS INSTRUCTION

*One night I dreamed I asked things of the Lord
And straight He answered me.*

DISCIPLE

MASTER, forgive Thy rash presumptuous one,
But in me is no rest if any word
Spoken by Thee sound harshly in men's ear!

THE MASTER

What troubleth thee?

DISCIPLE

                 Thy word concerning John:
Thou know'st he watched for Thee, with cryings strong
Besought God for Thy kingdom, taught all men
They must repent, prepare them for the Lord;
And on that day Thou camest, lo, he knew!
Proclaimed Thee, Lamb of God; chose for himself
To lessen day by day so Thou increase;
Knew Thee, the Bridegroom; all his joy to be
Friend of the Bridegroom, should rejoice for Him!

THE MASTER

Thou hast said well; all this the Baptist did,
And more thou know'st not of; was not My word,
No greater born of flesh hath ever been?
What wouldest thou?

DISCIPLE

       Master, Thou saidst of him
Another word: "Greater than John is he
Who least in the Kingdom is." What meaneth this?
Why then is John, who served as none besides,
Not in Thy kingdom, graced with highest place
At Thy right hand?

THE MASTER

       Thou know'st not what thou askest;
Nor understand'st conditions of the Kingdom;
Kings of the world give place to whom they will,
Invite within their borders, honours give,
As they shall choose. But, hast thou understood—
The Kingdom suffereth violence, the violent take?
See ye, they take; not God Himself bestows;
The Kingdom is no gift for easy souls
To get by grace of God. By force, a man
Must take and hold 'gainst multitude of foes.

DISCIPLE

But took not John the Kingdom? Thou, my Lord,
Art merciful! Wilt visit his offense,
And take Thy kingdom from him?

THE MASTER

        Nay, My son,
Not yet thou comprehend'st; I can, nor give,
Nor take away. Life, grace, the love of friends,
Honour and victory, praise, beauty, joy,
Virtue, and peaceful days—all these are Mine
To give My servant; this one thing alone,
The Kingdom, gets and keeps he by his prowess.

DISCIPLE

What, then, the Kingdom?

THE MASTER

      Where a King rules, is loved,
Trusted and served—the Kingdom. Though but one
Subject so hold him, yet is he a King,
King to that one; ten million subjects his,
Yet by himself doth each swear fealty
And pledge him to the King as though none else
Than he within the Kingdom; he must will
Steadfast allegiance through his life the pledge;
All else I give him; this must he bring Me;
Nay, might I give him the Kingdom, what were't worth,

The man a prisoner to his loyalty,
Not free to love and serve?

Disciple

                    Then, Lord, can he
Who wilful quits Thy Kingdom meek return?
The Master

Behold, I stand at the door to bring him in!
But who goes out is fenced about with foes
To hinder his returning; few there be
Who, going forth, have grace to come again,
And hard the way they tread!

Disciple

                    But, John, my Lord,
Returned not he to his old loyalty?
If John not in the Kingdom, who may hope?

The Master

And think'st thou lovest more than I? Canst trust
That I do watch and pray for them who err
As John hath erred? Thou, too, shalt pray and watch;
To know is not for thee; leave then the end!
No righteousness that man hath wrought is lost,
Forgotten before God! Many there be
Slow to believe in that they may not see,
Who yet are righteous; leave the rest to Me,
And know that love subsists eternally!

John gave Me love; and I, do I love less?
Why fear for him held in eternal love
And graced beyond others by My word, Well done!
Of what shall be, knows no man, not the Son!

Disciple

Forgive thy slow disciple, dull of heart!
They took thy word to John, and, all at once,
Conviction broke his heart, and to Thy feet
His alien thoughts, abased, crept sorrowful; —
He knew Thee, KING, and shamed him for his doubt!

VIII

A WOMAN ANOINTS HIS FEET

CHRIST sat at meat in Simon's house;
    (Man of repute was he,
    A righteous Pharisee);
And as they talked with noiseless step stole in
A woman known to men for shameful sin.

  Behind the Master as he half-reclined
    She came in lowly wise,
    With tears and piteous sighs;
She saw the blessed feet outstretched, had gone
With merciful sweet succour up and down,

  All travel-stained and marred with soil:
    One precious thing she had, —
    "My heart," she said, "be glad!"
Her alabaster cruse she brake, all sweet,
And spent the ointment upon His blessed feet!

  Softer than precious nard, her tears;
    She wept upon His feet,
    Nor thought her weeping meet
To wash the soil she rued; she loosed her hair
And dried with that poor glory men called fair.

  And while she reverent spilt her nard,
    Her tears let fall, her hair
    Used as a napkin fair,
Jesus nor spoke nor looked where she so wrought;
Nor seemed of her poor presence to take thought.

But Simon watched, and in his heart
    Conceived a thought of guile; —
    Would He let her defile
His person by unholy touch if He
Indeed that prophet He gives out to be?

No word he spake, but Christ perceived
    That thought he meant to hide:
    "Simon," Christ said to chide,
"Somewhat I have to say to thee, My friend;"
And Simon in his heart knew to what end.

His fear concealed, "Master, say on;"
    Courteous, replied the host; —
    "A creditor once lost
Sums by two debtors; one owed fifty pence,
Five hundred was the other man's offence.

"For they had nought to pay, the man
    Frankly them both forgave;
    Now which of these should have
Most love for him forgave them?" Simon said,
"He, I suppose, who most forgiveness had."

"Yea, thou hast rightly judged:" He turned
    To where the woman knelt,
    Bewraying all she felt
As o'er His holy feet her tears poured free:
"This woman whom thou know'st a sinner, see;

"Thy house I entered; no guest-rites
    Thou hastened Me to pay;
    No grace upon Me lay;
Not water for My feet, the common due
Of every guest, have I received from you.

"This woman with her tears hath wet
    My feet, and with her hair
    Hath wiped with tender care;
Thou gavest Me not the kiss for guest was meet,
But she not once hath ceased to kiss My feet:

"My head with oil didst not anoint, —
    Deniedst thy guest that sweet
    Refreshment in the heat:
This woman for My feet thought not too rare
The vase of costly ointment broken there!

"My debtors are ye both, but she
    Hath found the only way
    That debt she could not pay
To cancel in the eyes of Him she owed:
She loved much, and who with pains would goad

"His loving debtor? All her sins
    Forgiven her for her love,
    (Love hath its price above),
Clean goes she forth, from every stain made free
For sake of that great love she showeth Me.

"That other debtor, he who thinks
    His whole offence but small, —
    E'en though forgiven all,
Hath little love for the so generous lord
Blotted out his offences with a word!"

Then turned the Lord about and saw
    The woman, penitent,
    Her shamed face down-bent;
He said, — "Thy sins are all forgiven to thee,
For thou hast known much love to show to ME."

IX

Circuit in Galilee—Women Minister

BEHOLD the Master journeying to and fro
Through villages and cities, everywhere,
In Galilean borders: as He went,
With beauteous feet of Him who bears
    Good News
Upon the mountains and the plains, He taught,
And multitudes attended. Not alone,
The Lord; with Him the Twelve should be,
    with Him
And garner those seeds of life He dropped,
Ready for sowing elsewhere: here were, too,—
Going from place to place where'er He went,
Hearing those words that healed, seeing the
    grace
Of the Divine Compassion in His looks,—
Those Women, blessed above womankind
To be with Him, and hourly feed their souls
On words He spake! Nay, further were they
    graced;
To care for meat and drink fell not to Christ,
Nor were the Twelve encumbered to provide;
The women cared for these things,—happy, they!
The task they loved for sake of Him they loved
Fell to their lot, and of their wealth they gave
Things needful for the hour: now all of these,—
Mary called Magdalene, Chuza's wife
(He, Herod's steward, high in place and power),
Susanna, many others,—every one
Had by His word been healed of certain plagues
Destroyed her and oppressed:—would that we knew

The name of every blessed woman graced
To minister to our Lord; for us, to express
In grateful service of all she owed
To Him had healed her of infirmities,
Cast forth besetting devils, made her whole!
Ah, how would every woman joy to go
In train that followed Jesus, minister
Of all she had in thanks for great work wrought
For her and hers and all the sinful world!
All women born bless you, ye happy few,
Who did the part of all in Galilee!

BOOK II

PARABLES OF THE KINGDOM

X

Parable of the Sower

The Master sat by the seaside
And taught the folk. From far and wide
The people thronged the Word to hear:
They pressed him nearer and more near
The margin of the lake; a boat,
He entered, on the waves afloat,
And sat and taught the crowds immense
Gathered in expectation tense:
On all the upward sloping shore,
Vast sea of faces stretched before
The Lord as thus He sat. "Now hear,"—
Said He; and many things appear
Before them, set in simple tale,—
The Parable, which should avail
To exhibit truth to dullest mind,
As in a picture clear defined.

Behind the lake, beyond the shore,
Upon the loftier hill before
The Lord's uplifted eyes, He saw,
Perchance, a sower instant draw,
From script before him slung, the seed
And scatter it with little heed
Of ground whereon it chanced to lie:
With liberal hand he sowed, the event
Rested with Him the good grain sent.

To Him, who saw in things of sense
A likeness and a fond pretence
Of the eternal things He knew,
The Sower's act, and image true

Of that He came to do for men—
The seed to sow which should again
Yield hundredfold of living grain.

The sower, He said, went forth to sow
His seed, not careful where to throw
His handful, casting free around
On fertile as on barren ground.
Some fell on footpath trod by man
And beast, till hard as brick, it can
Offer no bed to hold the seed:
Thitherward flock the fowls to feed
On that not trodden underfoot
In the hard ground, wherein no root
Can strike, no stalk arise, to bear
In its due time the fruitful ear.

Now, here was rocky ground, whereon
Light lay the earth; the seed upon
This place fell too; nor long had lain
Ere, sprouted quick with sun and rain,
It showed full promising and green:
Alack, the roots, that part unseen
On which for life must plant depend,
Could not in shallow earth extend
To depth where they should moisture find:
Scorching upon the place now shined
The sun; the blade that had no root
Withered ere the time of fruit!

Among the brambles some seeds fell;
In fertile earth, these prospered well;
Down struck the root, up sprung the blade,
Fair promise its appearance made:
But, ah, good soil and sun and rain
Favoured the brambles as the grain,

And they, the hardier, stronger growth!
In early spring fast grew they both;
Then shoots and leaves the brambles spread
Crowding the blades, from overhead
Shutting out rain and wind and sun,
Choking that growth so well begun,
Till nought but brambles fed the soil,
And never crop asked reaper's toil.

Not wasted all the sower's seed;
On good ground cast with little heed,
Some grew and prospered every day;
The blade, the ear, full corn, display,
Each in its season, how good ground
Shall make the fruitful seed abound:
See you, some ears with weight are bent
Of hundred goodly grains,—one, lent;
The others, golden interest, brought
to him who sowed and him who wrought
The soil to rich fertility:
Less heavy other ears, but see,
In this one sixty well-filled grains
Rewarding all the farmer's pains:
In this, but thirty; would ye say,
Thirty for one, unworthy pay?

"He that hath ears, come, hear My word,
Pregnant with life when duly heard!"
The people pondered, knew the tale
A teaching tale for their avail:
But in that crowd all sorts of ground
The Lord had told of might be found.

XI

OF TEACHING BY PARABLES

CHRIST was alone, and to Him came the Twelve
With those most eager for His words: they ask,
"Why speak in parables to all this crowd?
Thy words so precious, Lord, dispersed are they,
Thy meaning wrapped in tale none understands;—
And, lo, thy sayings lost, as string of pearls
Dropped in the unstable, unconsistent sea!"
And spake the Lord: "Think not a man may learn
The mysteries of the Kingdom in short speech
To dullest, plain; nor think, to go and do,—
Sole obligation laid; no mysteries
To casual eye disclose them; these deep things
Pertaining to the Kingdom, how shall be
Unveiled the least of them to vision marred
And blurred by incessant glitter of the world!
But ye shall know, for ye the glamour left
Of things without, and came within that cool
And sheltered place the Kingdom is; to you,
Stone of a thousand facets shall disclose
Now these, and others now, as ye can bear:
But not in all eternity the whole
Splendour of Vision that God's Kingdom is
Shall be unveiled to one—for all have share!

"The rest that are without, how make them know?
Things daily manifest before their eyes
Leave them unseeing still: the natural world
Is full of parables for who can read:
Flying and running, birth and life and death,
Blood in the veins, sap rising in the tree,

Sun, moon, the night and day, the clouds and winds,
The rain and tender dew, the bow of hope,
Bridegroom and bride, intimate nuptial bond,
Children and father, friendship, city life,—
What each of these but symbol, shows one face
Of the incommunicable mystery,
Not to be comprehended by a man,
So infinite is it in blessedness,—
THE KINGDOM OF HEAVEN.

"See ye, as little child with spelling book
Finds nought but silly scratches on the page
Till teacher comes holding the magic key
Shall open knowledge—even so are ye
Till I by parable shall ope the world,
Disclose significance of common things,
Till, when by symbols few interpreted,
Men learn to read those books before their eyes,
Writ page by page, the mysteries of the Kingdom!
Who cannot will himself to will with power,
How can he hold without the will to hold
E'en that he hath already, how get more?
From out slack finger drops his little wealth,
And he who picks up what's in his way:
By this one law, the rich man richer grows,
Poorer the poor becomes; the good wise man
In wisdom yet increaseth; the sorry fool
Loses last grain of wit; who knowledge hath,
More knowledge wins, an ever swelling store;
And ignorance increaseth with the years:
This, too, the Law of the Kingdom; he who hath
Is more and more endued with that He hath—
Graces, gifts, powers and joys inherited
On entering the Kingdom; while slack soul,
Who willeth not to enter, loseth that
Of natural towardness he had before;

With every day more alien be his tastes,
Dull, his desires; he loseth that he hath!
Therefore teach I in parables; for see,
Isaiah's words, how well have come to pass,—
'Hearing, ye hear, and no wise understand,
Seeing, ye see, and shall no wise perceive: '
For greedy, gross, is waxed this people's heart,
Desiring that alone shall feed their lusts
Of flesh or spirit,—lusts of meat and pride.
Lo, therefor, deaf their ears to word of God
And closed their eyes to aught but prideful shows!
A blindness is upon them, their own deed,
And God's most righteous judgment; (for man's deeds
His judges be, and in correction smite):
Who would not see are blinded, nor can see;
Who would not hear, unabled they and deaf;
Heart cannot understand what neither eye
Nor ear conveys of the eternal truth.
How can these turn again as duteous sons
And cry on God to heal them when no word
Reacheth their understanding to convince?
Indurate to all parable, these judge
Themselves: and if they can, let them excuse,
And cry, 'Dark sayings, who can understand? ' "

So spake the Lord, mercy remembering
E'en in the act of judgment: who forgets
Truth that is wrapped in tale? This shall return,
Though trodden hard, or out of maw of bird;
Still living is the seed, and shall bear fruit
And after thousand years shall still bear fruit
A thousand and a thousand fold, those tales
Let fall by Christ on seeming-careless ears!
How wonderful are Thy judgments, Lord, Thy ways,
Past finding out! We, hard ones, how can we
Thy Mercy's tender wiles discriminate!

But "Oh," saith Christ, "blessed are your eyes which see,
Your ears, for indeed, they hear! No blessedness
Pertains to man so great as things to know
Which belong to his life. That mystery, the wise,
Sages and prophets, through all time have sought,—
That mystery's given to you to see and hear,
To handle with your hands of the Word of Life!
But those men, great in faith, saw not nor heard;
Or saw foreshadowings dim of the Event:
For you, fulfilment's kept.
                         This parable,—
See ye not what it means? then how can ye
Discern all parables, or how disclose
To men the inherent truth in all the shows
Environing them, that truth by which man lives?"

XII

THE "SOWER" EXPLAINED—1. *THE WAYSIDE*

THE Son of man goes forth to sow:
    The Word of God, the seed;
He scatters free with liberal hand,—
No sourest barren patch of land
    But gets a generous meed.

And souls, the soil in which He sows
    The good seed of the Word:
Ah, Lord, prepare that soil we be,
So, generous too, we yield to Thee
    Due fruit from seed interred!

Thou say'st, "Who understandeth not
    Is like a beaten way:
Satan swoops quick upon that thought,
Bare lying as a thing of nought,
    Cast out or gone astray:"—

"But, Lord, Thou speakest mighty words,
    Hard to understand;
While slow and dull of wit are we,
And scarce at all Thy truth we see
    For very light in flood!

"Have mercy on us, Lord, and spare
    For sins of ignorance!
How gladly would we understand!
Meekly we own Thy just demand,—
    Visit not our offence!"

. . . . .

"My child, thou comprehendest not
    That I demand of thee;
How couldst thou know the breadth and height
Of love and wisdom infinite
    Canst measure the wide sea?

"Seed of the Word dropped in a soul
    Creates an instant's stir;
Be thine to know if a life has come;
See thou cherish; give it room;—
    That nascent life, thy care!

"This, all the understanding thou
    Must bring to hear the Word:
A very fool guards bit and sup
Nor lightly oversets his cup;—
    So guard thou that thou'st heard!

"To receive the word that falls, thy part—
    Act well within thy power;
The seed must needs its due fruit yield—
So thou afford untrodden field;
    My covenant—sun and shower!"

But what should tread the field, my Lord,
    Laid open for Thy seed?
"Nay, many sowers go about,
Vain teachers all, an idle rout,—
    To these, if thou give heed,

"And make thy heart a market-place
    With stalls for every ware,
What growing place in thee is found?

Would any look that fruit abound
    On ground trod hard and bare?

"See then, My son, thou keep thy thoughts;
    Nor, easy—tolerant, let
Thy heart become a beaten way
Where vain conceits find place to play,
    But truth shall nowise set!"

XIII

2. *THE STONY GROUND*

A MAN there was who one day heard
With great delight that living Word,—
Lit up for him all common days,
Taught him to comprehend God's ways,
Gave peace in place of senseless strife,
And noble purpose to his life.

He heard and talked and grew apace;
With promise filled he all his place,—
As seed dropped where the sun's rays fall
And seasonable rains that call
Of early green, a quick display,
Promise of fruit some later day.

What if on rocky ground it fell,—
For all its promise, is it well
With seed in shallow soil that grows
Where stubborn rocks its roots oppose?
Who knows the word and does not love,
His show of growth is all—above!

The tender rootlets are not fed
From a full heart, nor nourished
On meditation, prayers and tears,
On loving hopes and tender fears,
On all that substance of the heart
In which the mind hath little part.

The man who was so glad to hear,
His show of life so quick t'appear,

Finds on a day that things go ill
With him would word of God fulfil:
His scruples stand in his own light,
Nor let him prosper as he might.

Nay, wiser men than he will flout
This very Word: Why such a rout
For hindrances in thine own mind?
If God there be, then is He kind,
Nor visits with a rigorous hand
Offense 'gainst even just command!

Half fearful, half persuaded, he
Will, now, with this, with that, agree;
Small persecutions soon assail;
His hold on truth doth not avail,
So shallow is the soil, to keep
A heart where is of love no deep:

So tribulation's winnowing flail,
Or persecution's fierce assail,
Shows this man's faith a passing phase,
Not rooted firm beneath his days!
He falls away, his promise green
Withered ere any fruit be seen!

XIV

3. *THE SEED AMONG THORNS*

THIS other man, he hath a heart
In which or wife or child hath part;
Neighbor or friend or public weal
Bears witness that this man can feel!

He hears the Word, and, lo, a shoot --
The love of God—takes deepest root!
He thinks upon the Fathers grace,
And tender tears bedew his face;

"Ah, make me worthy, Lord," he prays,
"To glorify Thy love with praise!"
So sprouts the seed, the roots strike deep—
Sure he will his fair promise keep?

Alas, he hath a hundred cares
Infesting e'en his secret prayers;
His wife—how make her worthy place,—
His child—how forward in life's race?—

His friends he makes his kind concern,
And for the common weal doth burn;
Riches and place, why, these he needs
To give due scope for his good deeds:—

Well-meaning, he, but every hour
Spent in pursuit of wealth and power—
How shall that seed to yield be brought,
Whose cult compels men's time and thought?

Anxieties and pleasures both
For God's sweet service make him loth:
With loving heart and willing mind,
Yet fails he to yield fruit in kind!

XV

4. *THE SEED IN GOOD GROUND*

THERE was a man who heard and thought;
Who in himself conditions brought
To foster that most precious seed;
His honest heart with reverent heed
Pondered the Word; he knew he had come,
With that blest Word, of life—the sun!

Now, good his heart as it was true:
Debased affections might not sue
Him from his part the Best had found:
His love, his service, gathered round
That living Word—his constant praise,
Guide, Light, and Comfort of his days!

No sudden growth marked this man's state,
Nor went he forth with joy elate
As one had found the good of life,
For whom no more are cares and strife.

Poor man, he waited many a day
Till plant of grace should fruit display;
A withered blade, an empty ear
Was all did to his sight appear!
Patient he waited still; said he,
"My punishment no fruit to see!"

But what is this? Unworthy seems
The life that he so fruitless deems;
This man, he knows, bears sixtyfold,
That other, thirty; sure, so cold

And barren soil for that blessed seed,—
His Lord's reproach is all his meed!

The Master walks abroad and sees
His drooping servant on his knees;
What weighs him down? A hundredfold
Of heavy fruit he scarce can hold!
See you, the fruit had grown, had borne
Full-ear the while the man did mourn!

XVI

OF THE HIDDEN LAMP

NONE brings lamp under bed to hide,
Nor under bushel lets it bide;
But, worthily on stand decrees
To place that light by which he sees.
Thou think'st to screen My word with care
Lest any see it shining there
In secret place of thy close heart?
The ostrich takes as wise a part:
Thou hast a secret none may keep;
The truth to all men's eyes shall leap,
And all the folk who pass thee by
Shall scornful to each other cry,—
"Lo, here a man who hath the light,
And thinks to keep it out of sight!"
Dishonour hath he done to Me,
And in men's eyes slight regard shall be,
Who holds the truth, nor makes it known,
As it were for his wealth alone.
The flame goes out, deprived of air;
And, live wick smothered, shall he dare
Move forward on his perilous way
Unlightened by that friendly ray?
Now let that man hath ears to hear
Exalt the WORD and have no fear.

XVII

Parable of the Tares and the Wheat

A MAN went out and sowed his field
With good seed, should large increase yield:
His devoir done, the good man slept;
Another, watchful, vigil kept,—
His enemy, who came by stealth,
Sowed pestilent tares where all that wealth
Of good seed waited sun and rain;
These came ere long the seed had lain,
And both seeds sprouted, wheat and tares,
In multitude, defying cares
Of anxious labourers to clear
The crop that cost their master dear.

They came before their Lord; said they,
"Sir, was it not good seed one day
Thou sowest in thy field? Then whence
Have tares come up for thine offence?"

The master heard, and taking thought—
"An enemy has this mischief wrought
To me and mine," he cried; said they,
"Wouldst have us gather them?" But, "Nay,"
Said he, 'together let them grow,
Nor try to weed out tares, lest so,
Ye wheat as well as tares uproot:
Let both together grow till fruit
Of wheat is ripened in the ear!'

"Lo, then, my reapers shall appear!
Then will I bid them, Gather first

The tares that spoil my crop; accurst,
In bundles to be burnt, these bind;
But every ear of wheat ye find,
Garner it heedfully, nor lose
A single grain of my just dues. "

The disciples heard and pondered long
How tares should get the wheat among,
And what the tares and what the field
And who the enemy concealed:
A symbol of the kingdom, knew,
But failed to read its import true:
Thrice happy men, these instant bring
To Christ their troubled questioning!
As soon as seated in the house—
"This parable explain to us,"
They cry insistent; He explains:
"The Son of Man sows the good grains,
The words of life, with earnest pains.
The field He sows is in the world:—
Wherever seed of truth lies curled
In sheltering folds of hearer's heart
Behold a man that hath his part,—
Son of the Kingdom who receives
That seed I sow and straight believes.
But there be other sons abroad,
Sons of that Evil One, whose word
Accuseth, hateth, ever lies!
These be the tares that strong arise
In field I purchase for mine own.
The devil, he this crop hath sown;
The wheat and tares alike are green,
Alike are goodly to be seen;
Both show alike the promise good
Of men's abundant wholesome food.

The harvest is postponed long;
Till end of world the reaper's song
Shall not be heard in field of Mine:
The reapers be Mine angels; then,
Shall they go forth to garner men;
Like as the tares burn in the fire,
So shall shrivel in the ire
Of the just Son of man who cause
Weak souls to stumble, men to fall
From grace of Him would save them all!—
Who scoff and doubt or souls offend
With evil courses to bad end.

As fiery furnace then shall burn
Their thoughts when they the truth discern
Impotent, they shall gnash their teeth,—
Perceiving all that grace beneath
Whose sheltering they dared transgress;
With cries and tears, they shall confess!
Meantime the righteous enter in
That KINGDOM they took pains to win.

"Who hath ears to hear, now let him hear!"
The Master cried; and holy fear
Possessed the hearts of all those men;
Might they be tares, could they again,
Despite of all His fostering grace,
Offend their fellows, bring disgrace
On Church of Christ,—by casual life,
By proud opinions gendering strife,
By holding up, men to mislead,
Alluring lights that dead souls breed?—
And each man questioned in his heart,—
Could his be this so shameful part?

XVIII

Parable of the Seed Growing Secretly

    The Lord said:—
God's Kingdom is as if a man
Cast seed upon the earth; none can
Do more than sow the goodly seed,
Then go his way, not taking heed:
He slept by night, and in the day
Worked he, or played, his wonted way.
But while the man forgat to look
The living seed its own way took;
He knows not how, but surely, lo,
He sees the seed spring up and grow:
Nor comprehends how germ concealed
In shrivell'd husk should be revealed
As the green blade, full ear of wheat,
As bread itself for men to eat!
See ye, the earth the secret holds
Of cherishing that she enfolds,—
The good seed fostered at her breast;
Sow ye the seed and leave the rest:
Think ye the Lord had not prepared
That soil in which His seed well-fared?
By storm and sunshine, rain and dew;
By drought and many labourers, due;—
When work of every worm, each nought,
Is to a sum of labour brought,
Lo ye, His earth, prepared to yield,
Is one prodigious fertile field!—
A field thou find'st it, very good,
With appetency fit endued,
All eagerly to take that seed

Thou scatterest with careful speed.
And, see, returned in season due,
A ripened harvest waits for you!
The earth herself hath known to bear,
First the green blade, and then the ear,
Herself hath known the fruit to yield
That, golden, gladdens all thy field.
Put in thy sickle straight and reap
A goodly harvest—thine to keep!

The disciples heard with joyful mind,
Relieved that they might hope to find
In hearts of men a ready soil—
Prepared of God through age-long toil
Of countless servants of His hand—
To take the Word at His command,
Bring forth and bear, to His high praise,
Fruit of good works and holy days:
For not a soul, from pole to pole,
But of this seed hath desperate need:
For never one but knows to hold
And bring forth fruit an hundredfold:
Their only business is to sow
With sedulous care, seed, needs must grow.

XIX

THE SEED GROWING SECRETLY—THE DISCIPLE

INFORMING the void silence, dropping Seed,
    I heard and did rejoice!
How apt thy word for my exhausted need,
    Engendering Voice!

My hungry famished soul puts eager forth
    Blind feelers for the Seed;
Sure, I would cherish till it yield due birth
    Grain that shall feed!

And day and night I wistful come to see
    A seedling that shows green;
Alas, no sign of things that virtuous be
    Is here, I ween.

Nay, worse; ill weeds do grow; good fruit is not;
    Or is not to be found:
Sure, seed of subtlest virtue can but rot,
    Lost in the ground!

Then I bethought me how in former days
    Like droppings had I heard;
And how I vainly watched for fruit of praise
    To prove the Word.

And is this sound, grateful as brave June rain
    To trees whose hands hang down,
But echo of desire? In sorry pain,
    I wept forlorn.

"Have faith," saith One; "thou heard'st the sowing; wait
    Till ripened in the ear,
Corn stand for cutting: take thy sickle straight,
    Reap, then, nor fear!

"The harvest shall be thine, and thou shalt see:
    The growing of the Seed
Is hid; a secret thou shalt leave with Me,
    And wait MY speed!"

XX

THE MUSTARD SEED

The Master paused, for in His eye
The Kingdom showed all gloriously;—
"Nay, how shall We make manifest
To weary souls the Kingdom's rest?
What parable to serve to show
How sudden its broad fields grow
Least seeds of virtue, germs of faith,
There where no harms have power to scathe?

"A man took grain of mustard seed
(So small a thing to take with heed!)
He sowed it in his field, and, lo,
E'en in a day he saw it grow;
Week after week it still uprose,
Higher than any herb that grows;
Still higher scales the air, and see,
That smallest seed becomes a tree!

"Its branches spread, great branches, they
Give shelter from the sun's hot ray;
From storm and tempest, see, they shield
The men and beasts are in the field:
In them the small birds sit and sing,
Seek here their nests on eager wing:—
This wealth of life doth all proceed
From that so inconspicuous seed!"

. . . . . .

The eager men thought they perceived
This tale of th' Kingdom them relieved
From anxious care lest seed, so small,
It scarce could yield a plant at all!
With joy beheld they least of seeds
Produce a tree for poor folks' needs,
Where sheltered souls sing blithe and play,
And rear up broods as glad as they!

The Church, the Kingdom is, and see,
A little word may bid it be:
It spreads and grows and fills the field
Which did one inch of surface yield
For its first planting: See, it thrives;
Men gather thick as bees in hives;
In 'ts branches, straight, they congregate
And bask them in so fair estate!

The Church itself, how small a thing
That day 'twas planted by the King!
Twelve Chosen Men the mighty band
Should carry Light to every land,
Should conquer kings, peoples restrain,
And, sin-diseased, make born-again!
The secret of their power, that Word,
Mighty to grow where it is heard!

XXI

The Hidden Treasure

Another likeness of the Kingdom, see;
And learn therefrom the part beseemeth thee:—

A man who dug his hired field
Lit on an unexpected yield,—
A buried treasure came to view:

Now covering up the place, he ran;
The worth of all he had, began
To reckon up, if it might do,

Brought into sum, to buy that field
Wherein the treasure lay concealed:
All summ'd, in anxious haste he flew

To buy the field, and count the wealth
That he had gotten (if by stealth):
Of all he had stripped bare, look you,

The man made rich by sudden find
Lives on his wealth with easy mind,—
His ancient labours left for new
And pleasant ways rich men pursue!

Disciples pondered: what may mean
This tale of field-trove never seen
Till a man laboured;—then gave all
So he might his that treasure call:
The treasure is the Kingdom, see,
All unexpected come to thee:

But not the while an idle mind
Goes sauntering, with no thought to find
Reward a labouring mind and heart
(Zealous to do their proper part),
Discover to the ravished eye!

But 'tis a treasure thou shalt buy
At price of all thou holdest dear:
Come, reckon up, and have no fear
Lest things thou leavest are worth more
Than this—must be thy single store.
There's ease and pride and joy of self;
And wilful ways and love of pelf;
There's flattery, and power and place
For who will join the eager race
To the world's winning post; there's sloth
To labours of the spirit loth;
Why, come to reckon up, there's all
The good I thought might e'er befall
Some lucky man who had his way;—
To part with all, and in one day!
'Tis hard, methinks, for a poor man
All he most blessed straight to ban!

. . . . .

HAST counted, soul, the other side,
The riches shall with thee abide
Then most, when thou forsakest most
Gains thou hast garnered at great cost?
The earth is thine, and all its wealth,
Sweet joys and pleasures for soul's health;
Solace of Strength to lean upon;
The grace of Goodness not thine own;

Alliance with the KING of Kings
WHO to thine aid His armies brings
In every moment of distress
When foes distract thee, ills oppress:
There's peace when all around is strife;
A child's glad-careless, happy life;
There's quick forgiveness for thy sin,
Ready or e'er thy prayer begin;
And, O, my weary-wandering soul,
There's One who hath the sole control
Of all thou art and all thou doest,—
Thy Master! whom to serve, thou must
At fixed "Attention" stand and wait:
No longer shalt thou runagate;
And, ah, what ease to be constrained
To hold that substance thou hast gained!

Make haste, my soul, compare and try,—
Sell thy poor dross, this treasure, buy!

XXII

THE LEAVEN

A BLIND man held it lightly in his hand—
The jewel that was left him, all his wealth;
Nor saw its radiance, knew its worth: with eyes
Impervious to the light, how see the glow
That little star gives out with every ray?
So found the Lord; how should He make men see,
The glorious, radiant Kingdom—dark to them,
A small thing, and opaque, of splendor shorn,
A little trifling toy not worth regard!

Another image took He: See yon dame
Mixing her bread in a trough; now she pours in
Water to hold the mixture consistent all,
And, kneading, to the oven straight conveys?
Heavy and flat, her bread, a weariness
To him who eats, not satisfied, but sad
With weight of food too leaden to digest!
But, no; she brings a little leaven forth,
Hides it in all that meal, and by-and-by,
She comes to mix, and lo, the whole is light!
Pleasant and good for food the bread she makes;
The man who eats goes strong upon his way.

The hearers pondered: What the leaven, then,
(And what the meal) a little in the midst
Will cause to rise, light bread to feed that flame,
A man's consuming life, from day to day?
The meal—is't all the loves and joys and hopes,
The passions and desires, fill that trough—
Man's heart, where he makes bread to live upon?

Without the leaven, all is heavy, flat,
Scarce to be eaten and endured as food,
And yielding nought to nourish the starved life?
And now, put in the leaven—hopes and joys,
Thoughts, works, desires and loves—why, how they rise,
A glad and light consistence, happy whole!
The leaven, sure, the very Word of God,—
Put in the trough of life transforms the whole
And turns the heavy stuff to wholesome food!
This, then, is like the Kingdom, how a man,
Receiving Word of God in the very midst,
His life is bound in one consistent whole
And he goes light; is bread that man may eat
And nourish soul upon:—Thy Kingdom Come!

XXIII

THE PEARL OF GREAT PRICE

A MERCHANT seeking goodly pearls went up and
    down the land,
And now and then a jewel rare came to his
    eager hand;
And here he sought, and there he bought,
    some pearl of value great;
And folk said of this wealthy man, How waxeth
    his estate!

But when the man sat down to scan the pearls
    he'd got with care,
Discerned he flaw in this one, stain or slight
    distortion there;
His soul in loathing turned away from all that
    goodly store,—
"O, found I but one perfect pearl, all these I'd
    hold no more!"

One day the news of such a pearl came to his
    ready ear;
He sought the man who own'd the pearl; in anxious
    haste drew near;
"Now, let me see thy jewel, hid in safe place
    and secure;
That better it be than mine own, I would full
    fain be sure!"

He gazed with vast cupidity on that mild-
    gleaming gem,
So large, so chaste, so perfect-pure! Abased, he

clasped the hem
Of th' owner's garment: "Now, declare," he
    piteously implored,
"If thou wilt sell this peerless pearl for all the
    wealth I've stored?"

Who owned the pearl gazed steadfastly, and thus
    at last he spake,
As one that scornful sets a task not one will
    undertake;—
"Go, sell thy goods, thy precious pearls, each
    costly thing thou hast,
With price of all these in thy hand, why, we
    may deal at last!"

The man went sorrowful, for joy he'd found in
    things he had;
How could he part with all that wealth had
    erstwhile made him glad?
Long he debated; should he sell, or keep those
    costly things?
The pearl persuades; he sells the whole, and all
    their value brings
To purchase that mild-lustrous gem: he holds it
    in his hand,
Takes it away with him, a joy, no man could
    understand
But who had sought for pearls of price, and knew
    to value each,
And knew that now he held a prize beyond
    hope's fondest reach!

. . . . .

So spake the Lord: disciples knew,—for
    little pearls they'd sought,
Small pearls of pleasure, profit, play, advancement,—
    easily caught
By any show of value in those trivial things
    they'd found;
And, now they knew their little worth, would
    trample on the ground!

For, happy men, disclosed to them that Pearl of
    price so great
The life of Him who offered it was added to make
    weight!
But not a gift, this pearl of price; a man must
    sell his all,
E'en to his secret thoughts, ere he that pearl his
    own may call.

At feet of Him who holds the pearl, his barren
    wealth must lay,
And stand, a poor man,—amply rich in that he
    bears away:
An image of the Kingdom see; learn how a man
    must trade,
Sell all he hath that he may buy that Pearl for him
    uplaid!

That merchant who seeks goodly pearls of wealth
    or place or name,
He, great of mind, of fortune great, an-hungered
    for high fame,
At feet of Him who is that Pearl, these must he
    haste to lay,—
A beggar seeking alms,—to go, a rich, rich man
    away!

XXIV

THE NET CAST INTO THE SEA

AGAIN the Kingdom is like net
Cast into the deep sea to get
What fish it meshes, without choice
Of good or bad; fishers rejoice
A heavy net to draw to beach;
Opened, alack, disclosed to each,
Are fishes of good sort and large,
But many fish must they discharge
In waste place of the world, for these
Too small, too vile in kind t'appease
The hunger of the meanest soul;
The good, in vessels place they whole,
The bad they cast away; for tried,
And wanting found, these must abide
Destruction, they must perish all,
E'en though caught in the net's great haul!

The Fishers four pricked up their ear—
They knew that net of which they hear
Now, for the second time: but, hark,
The Lord repeats not saying dark
Just as at first; new words hath wrought
Great thoughts within them, terror fraught!
What if the net they draw to land
Should furnish nothing for His hand?

Forthwith the Lord explains: ye say,
The Church hath sinners bad as they
That never in the net were ta'en;
Nay, worse are they, for they have lain

Safe in the net, as they were Mine!
Ye say, that holy souls must shine,
Convince you by their righteous ways,—
Then will ye come, nor make delays!
But, see ye, other is the part
That net, My Church, plays in the mart,
The field, the city, that wide sea
Wherein men cast that net for Me .
The bad and good are drawn within
And dwell together,—grace and sin!
Who knows but on some early day
The bad shall turn them round and pray?
But, pray they not, worse is their case
That wilful, they resisted grace!

Thus shall it be; the world shall end,
And that day I Mine angels send
To sever all those wicked souls
From them My righteous law controls;
They shall be cast to furnace flame,
Shall weep and gnash their teeth for shame!

Lord, if they weep, shall they do well?
Thy fire purgeth, prophets tell!

XXV

"Have ye understood?"

All day He sat by the seaside and taught;
Things hidden since beginnings vague of time
Disclosed He in dark sayings, parables:
As a man discovering glories of a land
Shows it in panorama, sheet by sheet,
Ever new landscapes, each more perfect-fair
Than that which went before, all various,
And every one delightsome, and all one—
That land delectable the traveller fain
Would show to homely folk who have not seen:—
E'en so, the Kingdom Christ unrolled that day
In many several aspects, so might eyes,—
Untravelled in the regions where is God,
To light of heavenly places all unused,—
Discern some glimmer of the radiancy,
Glad fruitfulness, fair justice, preciousness,
That is—the Kingdom! Weak, the eyes of men,
So every heavenly aspect, shrouded, shines
Through a dark saying few might comprehend!
Now, have ye understood these things? saith Christ;
"Yea, Lord," they answer; for the luminous words,
So simple, little child might understand,
Deceived the simple folk; they thought they knew,
Nor dreamed that each, dark with excess of light, —
Those parables the Master dropp'd as pearls!
Then sudden darkness fell; the folk dispersed,
Each to his habitation; idly told
Of lamp and net and leaven, common things,
A score,—on each the Master ready hung
An apologue good for the ear to hear!

But what might mean each story, mirror'd clear
On untroubled surface of their idle mind,
Concerned them not to know:—they went their way.

Ah, Lord, forfend that any word of Thine
Should glance thus idly from this heart of mine!

Not so the twelve Apostles; pondered they,
E'en through the long night watches. What might mean
Each transcript of the Kingdom, sudden flashed
'Fore unaccustomed eyes? What knew they now,
Unguessed before, about that mystery
The Kingdom of God—to be discerned alone
By instant beam illuming, here and there,
One single spot of that immensity,
Infinite, blissful, not to be known of men!
The words the crowd found easy, hard to these:
The more man knows, more strange the mystery grows.

Much pondering, a few things got they clear:
As palace of a king thrown wide to all,
The Kingdom is for who will enter in!

The Kingdom is a threefold mystery;—
Net, drawing bad and good, a field, with tares,
Agrowing 'mid the wheat,—the Kingdom, here,
That Church of Christ shall gather all men in!
But all men of that field bear not good fruit:
The faithful heart, the second mystery,
That holds the Kingdom its one precious pearl
For which all loss is gain. Have I sold all?
Am I indeed good ground? The anxious soul
Queries persistent of its patient Lord:
But not so much as this the soul shall know
That in the Kingdom is:—Believing, go,
And growing secretly, till that last state,

The final mystery man may not conceive!
See, graced to sudden mighty growth that seed
Ye go to scatter free in all the world!

Thus dimly with uncertain eye they spell
Those mysteries of the Kingdom Christ had taught:
But not one word these men let idly slip;
For each, a treasure pondered in his heart,
As good maid ponders speech of him she loves!
And this His word to them: Now, go ye forth,
Disciples of the Kingdom; rich are ye
As householder with many good things stored;
Bring forth things new and old for him who comes
Hungry, to share thy ample plenitude,
Athirst, to taste what wine of life thou hast!

XXVI

His Mother and His Brethren

A WHISPER passes slow from mouth to mouth,
From row to row, of them who sat and heard,—
Vast multitude of eager listening folk;
Man charged with message pulls his neighbor's sleeve;
He twitches man in front and mouths the words
His fellow passed to him; quick frowning brows
Query, impatient, what 'tis all about,—
This interruption, impertinent:
At last a man stands up and cries aloud,—
To stop this murmuring unbearable
To the tense listening crowd—"Thy mother waits
Thy mother and Thy brethren fain would speak
A word with Thee, they stand without."
                                            Remote,
On the far edge of all that breathing throng,
The little family group impatient fret
That He, their very own, should give Himself,
Unheeding all their claims, to public use:
Wise in their generation, they forsee
Trouble will come of popularity
They, jealous, eyed, nor understood at all!
Impotent, they assert a right to stop
The SAVIOUR OF THE WORLD in that slow work
Wrought line on line for man's Salvation.

Sure, He who taught men goodness would show forth
All a son's duty, all a brother's love?
But there be nearer ties than kith and kin;
The truth that a man lives by, more to him
Than dearest bond of mother, wife or child;

New law of spirit-kindred speaks the Lord,
Relationship within the Kingdom's bounds
Reaching to none outside, nor mother dear,
Nor wife nor tender child; but, ah, enhanced
A thousandfold, the love that binds these close, —
Included in the Kingdom!
                         He answered straight,—
Who is My mother? and My brethren, who?
And looking round on them that sat about,
He lowers His hand toward them, His followers,
Disciples of His choice;—Behold, saith He,
My brethren, these, My mother, all My kin!
For see, we be, all ye and I, one kin;
One Father own we,—Him which is in heaven,
And all our part, to do our Father's will:
That will, came I to manifest to men,
And whoso hearing hastes My Word to obey,—
That man, My brother; woman, sister dear!
The will of God, the one strong law of men;
Obedience, sole tie of tenderness
Shall outlast flesh and blood, proclaim to men
Paternity divine of sons of God.

XXVII

"The same is My Mother"—The Disciple

All his rest is on her arm;
She, his only shield from harm;
She doth his sole meat supply;
All his joy is in her eye.

Helpless, that is not his care;
A burden, she is strong to bear;
Fragile, will she not forefend?
Ailing—soft, her love shall tend.

Jesus, Saviour, Son of man,
Who camest, Infant of a span,
Was Mary Thy one Mother mild,
Or art Thou ever born a Child?

My trembling heart doth in me burn;
There, perchance, shall I discern—
Though the stall be all defiled—
The tender form of Christ the Child:

Is there One, a little One,
Who lieth sweetly as a son—
All His meat, the Father's grace
All His joy, the Father's face;

Rueing not His feeble state,
Fearing not the ills that wait,
Safe, nor asking why, nor how—
Jesus, then, not I, but Thou!

Other fearsome inmates there;
Evil dragons, giant Care;
Hope, joyous, sees them led in thrall,—
This "Little One" shall rule them all.

XXVIII

Rejected

NEW lessons duly given, new work done,
The ten great Parables, as planets, shot
From the hand of Him who made, to run their course
Eternal in those heavens where souls of men
Seek light of star to guide; finished, this work—
Perfect and very good—the Lord departs.

Wistful o'er them of Nazareth, pleasant folk,
Around whom cling all memories of youth,
He thither goes with train of loyal men,
Disciples, with their Lord. The Sabbath come,
Again He teaches in their synagogue;
Again, they wonder at the mighty words
Proceeded from His mouth: alack, the day!
What hostile power compels that men repeat
That error has condemned them? Astonished, they,
But not to their salvation: "Pray, who is this
That comes amongst us with such might words?
Where hath he learned this wisdom? Bears it seal
We recognise, of doctor of the law?
And by what right performs he mighty works
Unauthorized of our rulers? Year in, year out,
Have we not known him well, a working man,
A carpenter who did small joiner's tasks?
His mother, too, is she not Mary called,—
James, Joseph, Simon, Judas,—all we know,
His brethren, sisters, too, belong not all
To family of decent working folk
Here living in mean street? Pray, who is this
Assumes to teach his betters, would know more

Than scribes and doctors teaching in our midst!"
Just indignation filled them, as when one
Teacheth new doctrine, credentials having none.

Offence they take, and Jesus tells them why:
Ever He placeth finger on the spot
Where lurks disease; a principle reveals
To guide those men and all men in like case:
What His offence? That He belonged to them:—
"No prophet in his own country shall find grace;
Strangers shall hear his word, but not his own;
No honour hath he of his kith and kin,
Of them in his own house; not there his work
Of saving grace and service shall he do;
For none can work beyond the measure strait,
His fellows grace him with of generous trust."
Poor city, Christ went forth and did no works—
Save that He laid His hands on few sick folk—
So hindered Him, these men, by unbelief!
He, who knew man, astonished went away
At the great marvel of their vast unfaith;
How could they see and hear nor know the truth!

Why are those bristles in a man erect
Against that neighbor, better than the rest,
Not yet due stamped with hall-mark of the world?
The world approving, we delight to praise;
His glory makes us great; meantime, we wound
With unbelief, contempt, a thousand pricks
That neighbors know to make their neighbor smart.
Is't envy that consumeth all our power
Of upright judging, knowing what is true?

Neighbor to every man, the Lord remains;
Still are we envious of His place and power,
His right to lead us, utter the last word

In all conflicting cries that vex our days!
A man like us, men say, what doth He know?
What right hath He to order wiser thought
Than any man discerned in those dim days
When Jesus walked the plains of Galilee?
Offended at Him, and turn deaf ear!

Still wistful, waiteth He our slow relenting,
And meantime He can do no mighty work,—
Sudden uplifting of all people's hearts—
Hindered, His grace, by our crass unbelief!
A penny piece shall hide the orb of day,—
Our little faithlessness put out our SUN!

XXIX

HE COULD DO NO MIGHTY WORKS THERE

AND is it true He doth no mighty works
In this our England, grown so scantly dear
To the cold sons she nurtures at her breast?
Where be the men of might, the giant race,
Who did great things in our midst! Now, where be they
Whose pulpit thunders shook a nation's soul?
Or they, sweet souls, who filled a little space
But walked with God, and sang, and still their song
Droppeth as dew on souls dried up and sere?
Tinkers enow have we, but where that one
Who knows to mend a broken Pilgrim's heart
So it shall hold the red wine of God's grace?
Do poets "justify the ways of God"?
Who painteth a great picture, men shall bear
With allelulias through their crowded streets
For its witness to th' ineffable mystery—
All the world's wonder—Immanuel, Virgin-born?
Where be the willing folk who bring deft hands,
Wrought stone, or wood, or vessel choice of gold,
To raise a sanctuary shall for ever show
That, there, the centre of the people's life?
Do mighty voices shake our Senate House,
Enunciating, not expediency,
(Vain god we bow before,) but principle,
Pure patriot-principle, sure word of God?
These have been; are they now?
                              Who tells a tale
Shall open all men's eyes to see the way
Men work on men, and nature lays cool hand,
And God holds every issue,—tho' the NAME

Be little named on the pleasant page?
Who rears his child to know that one sole aim
Shall dominate his days; for God, in God,—
His steadfast purpose, his supremest joy?

Not gone are they, the mighty works of old;
Latent they lie, as Sleeping Beauty bound,
Till magic kiss of faith shall wake them up;
Then, see—they stir, they rise, stretch hands, try strength,
Ope eyes and go forth, strong and fair to bless
Mankind,—those mighty works our God doth keep
Sealed 'neath His hand till men shall come in faith!

We cry on Thee, our Lord, increase our Faith!
Bid us from quest of her we call "the Truth"—
Vain births of scalpel, microscope, and text
Minute-dissected till its life evade
Hard methods of the scholar. These be true;
True, gutter-children speak unseemly words;
But, therefor, childhood is unlovely? No!
True, there be pimples on an aged face
Which art may picture all a pimple-patch
Nor see the beauty life and thought have wrought;
True, textural error may impugn a phrase;
These things be true; but make not that full-orbed
And radiant Splendour we may name, The Truth—
Proportion is whose essence, faith whose life,
An all-embracing wisdom, whose content,
And CHRIST, her sole Embodiment!

BOOK III

ADMINISTRATION OF THE KINGDOM

XXX

HE STILLETH THE STORM

EVEN was come upon a day
When Christ had laboured long; alway,
Multitudes pressed to hear Him speak
Or healing from His hand to seek.
Outwearied, entered He a boat;
The disciples, ever quick to note
Each indication of His will,
Quick followed Him: there's wind to fill
Sails of the little craft; saith He,
"I would from all folk be free
A little space, repose to take;
Go we to other side of lake."
E'en as He was, they took Him then,
And launched the boat, those fisher men:
(Some other boats were with Him there;
Sea-wise, would they that crossing dare?)
Scarce had the skiff got under weigh
Than sleeping in the stern He lay,
His head upon a pillow low—
Poor couch, His friends had made Him so.
Now, black the restless waters grow
'Neath clouds as black; the wild winds blow
With steady stress from angry skies:—
Such sudden squalls must needs arise
In mountain lands; and neighbors told
Of awful risks to those o'erbold.

The skiff leaped high, the skiff sank low;
"Sure that will waken Him!" but, no;
He lay serene in slumber bound,

Through strife of elements around.
Great storm of wind upon the sea
Their vessel filling, "What doth He
Asleep, while we, in jeopardy?"
Half-angry, cry they, yet refrain
From rousing Him for all that strain.
At last, they venture; scarce can they
Get at Him for the monstrous fray
That winds and waters wild create;
They wake Him, —soon 'twould be too late!
"Our Master, hast Thou then no care
That we are battling 'gainst despair?
Thy love goes sleep, nor shields us, poor,
Who for Thy sake the storm endure!
Save, Lord, we perish!" Lo, He wakes,
And first, that storm of fear that breaks
Tumultuous through their cries and fears,
He chides, or o'er their prayer He hears—
Grants peace from tumult of the storm
Whose perils, sure, excuse alarm!

Then, He arose, where none could stand,
And issued, kingly, His command:
"Peace!" saith He, and the waters drop
To their low level; rude winds stop:
And a great calm falls all around—
A stillness, wonderful, profound,
So men might hear the Voice of God
Control rebellious storm and flood!
"He stills the raging of the sea!
His servants, floods and tempest be!"—
Frighted, exceedingly, they cry,
Those men who saw their God so nigh!
"Who then is this?" they fearful ask,
"Who bringeth winds and seas to task
And they obey His potent word—

As children by command deterred
From small rebellion, little flight
Of mischief's furtive fond delight? "

Rough winds, wild waves, sank soft to sleep
At word of Him who knows to keep
These in the hollow of His hand,
Obedient to His least command.
These were rebuked, nor these alone;
The disciples heard His awful tone:—
"Why are ye fearful?", asked the Lord,
"Not yet know ye to trust My word?
Not yet are certain I command
Those adverse powers on every hand?
Not yet assured that I fulfil
For least disciple all his will?
Why should ye fear, when I refrain
The hearts of princes, winds restrain?
Have I then taught you all these days
Nor know ye the first word of praise,—
That trust in Me, that mighty faith
Which knows not fear in life or death?
My labours, have they been in vain,
That ye no certainty attain?
Turn back, poor souls, and learn ye well
Faith's earliest rudiments to spell!"
Like chidden children, low and meek,
The disciples find no word to speak!

We know the tale; have we not quailed
A thousand times when fears assailed,
When all our sky is overcast,
Nor spot of standing-room, earth-fast,
Might our wild staggering steps sustain—

Ah, then, 'fore God, how we complain!
"Nay, tell me not a God of love
Ruleth men's fortunes from above!
I, but a man, would never, sure,
Let them I love like ills endure!
Then if a man be tenderer far,
What proof have I that God doth care?
Nay, I will call on Him and cry—
'Is't nought to Thee that I should die?' "
Of "little-faith," we speak this word,
And through the din a voice is heard:—
"Peace," restless tumult of wild cares,
"Be still," ye dreadful fears, despairs;—
And suddenly we are isled around
In God's peace, infinite, profound!
Those things we dreaded cease to vex,
No perils, tumults, more perplex
To the dear feet of God we come
Like timid children afraid to roam.

To whom then spake the Lord that word of peace,
So sudden soothed the sea, bade storm to cease?
Could the insensate waters hear His word,
The winds, are they by utterance deterred?
Or hath He given a word, mystic key—
Which opes an instant's space, that we may see
Mystery of things unseen,—"the Prince of powers
That hold their sway in air?"—This world of ours,
Is it administered by myriad sprites
Lab'ring for man's diseases or delights?
Be these, the angelic host His voice obey,
And those, the wilful spirits of decay
Who haunt waste places, bid Malaria breed
And waste with horrid pains the human seed;
Who in our dense-thronged cities find a place
Where they make free to decimate the race;

Who vex the seas, consuming fires, fan;
And move unstable earth to 'whelm vain man?
Be these the secular works of them whose choice—
Obedience to an evil Father's voice,
Whose works they do; and, labouring at his hest,
Continually the sons of God molest
E'en as they did while earthly frame they wore,
In mischiefs yet increasing ever more?
Was it to these Christ spake, and all was still,—
For these, unwilling servants of His will,
Compelled to do His pleasure? All the harms
With fell care they accomplish, dire alarms,—
What do they all but summon to the fight
Strong Daughter of the heavens, Science, hight?
See how her Knights go forth in eager haste
To combat unseen dragons of the waste!
See how they fall and die, one, two, a score,—
Science, uncowed, but sends forth Knights the more!
Full fell the conflict; victory is sure,
For Knowledge, born of Him who doth endure,
Knows no relaxing, failing, in her course,
No pity hath she, knoweth not remorse;
Toward noxious things, Destruction is her name;
For whatso worketh benefit, this same
Servant of God, as Progress, shows to men,
Beneficent in action: every ill,—
Unwilling instrument to work His will!

They who worked ill, hap, evil works still do,
Divested of the flesh; but these—the few
Be they, or many—ever gathering host,
Whose days are spent in seeking out the lost,
In serving Christ in ways Himself made plain,
What state of blessedness do these attain?
Sure, their works follow them; they still go on,
Still wait their Master's word,—"Servant, well done!"

And, cities many under each one's hand,
Sweet graces work they at divine command!
There be the flowers to cherish; fair trees, shield
From mischief gnaws their vitals; make corn to yield
Due bread for men; the sick at heart and sad
With unseen ministrations to make glad;
To carry on in ways these had designed
The works good men, perforce, had left behind;
Poor wandering souls they hasten to retrieve,
With whisper of love's Sesame,—"Believe."

What next, we know not; whether grace of God
Will conquer all vexed spirits of the flood—
All waves of the world which we misname our life—
And bid them cease from tormenting and strife,
Allay their fever in that sea of peace
Where e'en the wicked shall from troubling cease,—
This may we hope from Him whose name is love!
Meantime, we know that Voice, uproar above,
Nor dare disquiet us, how rough the sea,
Lest He should chide our faith's inconstancy!
"What stuff is this!" saith one who knows the hour,
And how, as long ago, fair Nature's power
Is dominant and sole o'er land and sea;
And man's whole part, to learn how those things be,
She, cunning, doth combine and bring about!
"Science, our sole deliverer from doubt;
And all her work, to watch the subtle ways
Nature employs. What room for spirits, then,
The souls, forsooth, of good or evil men!"

"Nay, but, have souls no part in scheme ye praise?
What's flesh? Slight curtain drawn to screen the light
From soul, would not in th' open of men's sight
Its secret energizings manifest;
But Soul, (or mind, or principle you choose,)

Lays herself out that 'Nature' she may use
To turn her wheels, her ships to carry straight,
To yield her triumphs, till she soar elate,
Sole-sovereign of that Sovereign rules the earth!

"Why, yes; in mind of man must come to birth
Due recognition of those laws benign,
Once learnt—and man's estate is half divine!
But, see, that body ye despise, the mean
Whereby we contact reach with things unseen—
Those very laws that rule us! Naked Soul,
How shall it 'stablish contact with the whole—
How, smallest lens or wheel in right place set?
How, power to move least mote of matter get?

"Lo, there, the mystery! That day we find
How a man's hand is governed by his mind,—
The Tree of Knowledge in our garden-plot
Shall grow for our using: miracle is not
For him who knows how spirit, matter, rules;
Till then, we ponder, test—and own us fools!
Who knows but Death, a higher state, may yield
That knowledge to our searching not revealed;
And naked Soul be free to work its will—
Or, mountains move, or bid wild waves be still!"

XXXI

THE DEMONIAC IS RESTORED

THEY reach the other side, and, on low strand,
In country of the Gerasenes they land;
Come down to meet Him, see, terrific sight,
Man naked, savage, fierce,—a sorer fright
To the disciples than the storm, allayed
By word of Him who "Peace," on instant, bade:
But, here, a soul tossed by its secret pains,
Not to be held with fetters; iron chains
Asunder rent he; no man's strength could hold
This wretch who night and day, through heat and cold,
Made awful wastes more hideous by his cries,
Gave terror to the tombs, where, see, he plies
Sharp stones upon his flesh, and cuts and tears;—
And fearful shepherds from that region scares!

And, lo, the man saw Jesus from afar,
Cried out and ran and fell,—but knew a bar
"Twixt him and the Son of Man: "What then have I
To do with Thee, Thou Son of God most high?
Let me alone nor torment with the sight
Of all Thy grace! By God, I Thee adjure,
Leave me at large to wait the issue sure
Of Thy last judgment! Why, before that day
Wilt Thou torment us? Prithee, go Thy way!"
For Christ addressed Him to that power within
Which drave the man to raging, rebel sin.
"Come forth." He bade, "spirit unclean and vile,
Whose constant lust is to destroy, defile!
What is thy name?" And, cowed, he made reply:
"Legion, my name, for many devils cry

And rage in this one soul given up to us:
Nay, send us not away, but bid us thus;—
Say, get ye to that herd of swine ye see,
Enter to them, and let this man go free!"

He gave them leave; and all the herd, distract
By strange unease, put their brute strength in act;
In sudden violent rush vent their distress,
And plunge from precipice, hot-foot to press
To the cool waters of the sea for ease
From intolerable burnings of disease.

The men who fed them haste with panic tale
To their masters in the city. "What avail
To feed and guard the swine when one doth come
Able to 'gulph two thousand in that tomb
Of the deep sea whence none shall be restored?
The man possessed with devil, sane is he,
But at what cost—nay, come ye out and see!"
And all the city came to see this thing—
How rebel spirits succumbed to the King!

There, terror of those wastes, the man sat low
At feet of Him who had subdued him so;
Sat clothed (in garments the disciples lent?)
Restored to sense and goodness, solely bent
To keep him in the presence of the Lord,
Knew to deliver him with potent word!
And were these glad to see their brother healed,
To see that urgent need of men revealed—
The Power could reach th' ultimate source of sin,
Spirits of evil let to rule within?
Knew they no hellish promptings in their heart
That they dared pray Him from their coasts depart?
Did no good angel hold them from that prayer
Of whose presumption hardly were they 'ware?—

Who held them from their gains—an enemy,
Himself by right should perish in that sea!

And Christ—the Saviour, yielded to their fear,
For never prayer falls idle on His ear!
The Gerasenes' inhospitable land
Affords no spot of earth where He might stand
To heal and teach and bless that barbarous race:
Rejected,—meek, took boat to quit that place!
But who is this in haste and all distraught,
With love and terror torn, urgent besought
That he might be with Him who knew to save!
The Lord regarded with look, steadfast, grave,
This new disciple; faith and love discerned;
Knew how great longing for His service burned
In that poor soul late outcast of his kind:
"Return," saith He, "to home and friends, and find
Amongst thine own how best thou shalt serve Me;
Declare to them how God hath dealt with thee!"
Now, will this man respond to that sure test
Christ offers to each disciple—laying hest—
A task of lesser things, on him would great
Love-task for Him perform? The man went straight
To his own city; published 'mongst them all
How Christ alone was mighty to enthral
Legions of rebel spirits, cast them out:
This told he in Decapolis, round about
Coasts of that land which had the Lord refused,—
And set men marv'lling while the tale they mused.

Why, here a tale to scoff at! All men know,
Science the story flouted long ago!
A joke, forsooth, that devils should on swine
Spend their fine spirit-essence, half divine;—
That there be devils, spirits, Power to deal
With that which no man can see or feel!

"Nay, we be flesh and blood: we comprehend
Such things as reason sanctions; let us end
Vain talk of devils, spirits of the air
Able to reach our sprite, its motions, share!
That which we see, believe we, right or wrong;
The rest hold we but as an idle song!

In sooth, we know not; nought can answer these—
Accept, reject, with unconcern and ease!
Like him went down to Ethiopia, we,
Bewildered, read, nor can the meaning see:
This thing we know: In that tumultuous scene,
Our Master moveth Godlike, kind, serene:
He seeks no audience, asks no ready praise,
Concerns Him not to justify His ways;
Rejected for His grace, He makes no plaint,
But tender-wise, lays He the soft constraint
Of His command upon the man He freed
From awful bondage: this, our simple creed,—
None other than the Christ hath been conceived
By genius, or of credulous souls believed,
Could move through like wild scene with grace benign,
Transcendent in simplicity Divine!

Not we, what moves the strong demoniac, know;
Like figures skating on thin ice we go;
Speak of the weather, that man's easy gait,
That other,—awkward; sorry we were late!—
Sudden, a crack! quick sinks our airy grace,
Submerged in that cold dread Unseen!—No place
We found; for in our cheerful hours,
Condemned we as illusion, fear of powers
Ill of intent who labour to destroy;—
We chose the pleasant paths and shunned annoy!

This other thing we know: In awful hour,
Consumed of passion, hate, wild lust of power,
Our raging spirits tear their heedless way
To end we covet, scorning reason's sway;—
Sudden, we hear a word—"My son, be still!"
And all that tumult succumbs to His will:
Humbled and sorrowful, we seek our place
At the dear feet of Him whose Godlike grace
Subdued demoniac more wild than we,
And bade him forth—Christ's messenger to be!

XXXII

THE MAIDEN RAISED—THE WOMAN HEALED

THE little maid was sick; how fair she lay,—
Her beauty quick-consuming in decay!
Father and mother hung o'er their one child,
Refraining for her sake their 'plainings wild:

Then one came in and spake of Jesus' power,
Said, He was nigh at hand that very hour—
"Go, fetch Him to the house!" the mother cries;
And spurred by eager hope the Father flies:

Ere very long he met Him on the way,
But hemmed in by vast crowd; what hope to say
That potent word, a father's passionate prayer,
Should move Him to compassion? How declare

To Him, in midst of multitude, how dear
The little daughter, lay to death so near!
But now, Jairus presses through the crowd,
Falls low at feet of Jesus, cries aloud,—

"My little daughter is at point to die,—
"E'en now she might be saved, wert Thou but by!
Come, haste Thee to the house kind hands to lay,—
With healing touch drive fell disease away!"

The Master said no word, but rose and went;
Disciples, multitude, with one consent
Pressed on and thronged the Saviour; lo, a pause,—
Christ Jesus stopped and cried—(now what the cause?)

"Who touched my garments " All the crowd denied,
And Peter, ever forward, stood and cried,—
"Master, Thou seest men throng Thee round about,
Why askest then who touched Thee?"—"From without,

One touched, for virtue hath gone forth from ME:"
Then looked He round that trespasser to see:
A woman, trembling, shamed, her act revealed,
How she had dared to touch Him and—was healed!

For twelve long years—the time the child had seen
All her glad days—had this poor woman been
Deprived of joy in living by disease;
Of means to live, drained by physician's fees!

She heard of Him nor money asked nor price;
Secret, contrived a woman's sly device;
"For if I can," saith she, "but touch the hem
Of His garment, lo, a single touch shall stem

Tide drains my life away!" So she drew near,
Touched, and was healed: but durst not, she, appear
Before His face to own the thing she'd done;
And healing got she as by stealth alone!

A hungry man snatches a loaf and flies,—
But had he waited, seen the kindly eyes
Of liberal baker on his famished face,
He had been bold to ask a loaf, of grace,

Not furtive steal it, adding shame to need:
And this the lesson the dear Lord took heed
To add to healing the shamed woman took,
The while love waited for her in His look!

Then gently, "Daughter, be thou of good cheer,
Thy faith hath made thee whole; go home, nor fear!"
"Daughter," saith He, "so worthless I, and bad!"
His word beyond His healing made her glad!

Meantime the ruler waited, hot in wrath;
Now who was this presumed to cross his path?
Sudden his anger cooled; from house one came—
"Why troublest thou the Master? All's the same

To her thou lovest if He come or stay;
Thy daughter's dead, her spirit passed away!"
The Lord, who knows the ache of every breast,
To sorrowing father word of cheer addressed,—

"Nay, heed not what they say; do thou believe,
And, lo, thy living child thou shalt receive!"
As they draw near the house, the mourner's cries,
Sombre and shrill, from stricken home arise:

The crowd urged forward, but the Lord forbade:
His four disciples only with Him stayed,—
The maiden's father, mother, these the few
Suffered by Him about as near He drew

To th' young dead maiden. Shrilly flutes annoyed,
The crowd's loud mourning tumult, peace destroyed!
"Give place," saith He, "why make ye this ado?
The child but sleepeth; she shall wake anew."

They laughed in scorn, knowing she was dead.
He put them forth, and drawing near the bed,
(Only the maiden's parents standing by,
And the four who followed Him): "Maiden, 'tis I,

Who come to bid thee rise!" He took her hand,
So tender to the tender maid, bade, "Stand!"
Her spirit come again, she rose and stood,
Lifted her eyes in hardly conscious mood,—

Whence had she come? What wonders might she tell
To her rejoicing parents, how there fell
Upon her ear, removed from sounds of earth,
Voice able, there, her spirit to bid forth

From where is never substance, touch or sound;--
Frail voyager come back from the Profound
Where spirits be, to take her place again,
A little daughter in the homes of men!

But He was there Who called the darling child,
Assured already by His aspect mild:
He bade them give her tender care and food;
And while He blessed the child, her parents stood

Astonished out of measure at the might
Of Him had known to summon from the night
Of awful Death their Daughter!—"See ye keep
A secret, how the maid was waked from sleep!"

Shall we wake up, dear Lord, and find Thee there—
Uplifting naked Soul with tender care?
If death be but a tryst we keep with Thee,—
Lo, we are coming, Lord, our babes and we!

XXXIII

Two Blind Men Restored, and the Dumb Made to Speak

Never to see the redness of the dawn,
    The tender hues of eve;
    Never perceive—
From all that knowledge comes of sight, withdrawn—
    When friends do grieve;
Or, be there with happy smile on face we love,
    How shall joy move
Our fellowship when we no sign may see?
In desolate places must the blind man be.

This blind man hath a brother found, one blind
    Like him, shut out from sight
    Of all delight;
Like him, alone amongst his friendly kind
    Who see the light!
Together make these their own little joys;
    Escape annoys
In talk of all those things that move a man's heart
Then most, when he from others goes apart.

To-day, great news stirs those two lonely souls;
    Friends give them news of One,
    Great David's Son,
Who all afflictions of mankind controls,
    Speaks, and 'tis done!
The blind go seeing and the deaf men hear!
    "Nay, then, shall fear
Keep us from Him the King of men, so great,
Alone, He rules man's intimate estate!"

Lo, He comes by! They follow—cry on Him;
      Eager and loud they cry,
      Lest He pass by,
Nor ever hear their voice nor know how dim
      To sightless eye
Are all the delights of beauteous world He made!
      "Have mercy!" said
The two blind men—His Mercy all their plea,—
"Have mercy, Lord, and bid thy servants see!"

Entered the house had Christ, and bade them rise:
      One question asks the Lord,—
      "Think ye My word
Is able to give sight to darkened eyes?"
      The blind men heard;
With leaping heart together they cried out
      Without one doubt,—
"Yea, Lord, we know that Thou canst bid us see!"
"According to your faith, so shall it be!"

He touched their eyes—so potent and so kind
      A touch, sure never fell,
      So soft a spell,
So quick, as made to see these two poor Blind!
      Ah, it was well
With them that day when seeing, forth they went
      And knew Christ sent—
Deliverer of poor souls in darkness lay,
That they might share the gladness of the Day!

One other prisoner groaning in the pit,
      He passeth in His way;
      The light of day
This man perceives; but silent he must sit,
      Nor word can say
Of thoughts all turned to bitterness that surge

   And utt'rance urge
Of his sealed lips: Christ's pity set him free!
"He makes the dumb to speak, the blind to see!"—

Cried out the marvelling multitudes amazed,—
  "Our fathers never saw
  Since came the Law,
Prophet could thus set captive prisoners free!"
  To Thee draw me,—
We who go blind to Thy sweet ways of grace,
  Nor see Thy face,
Nor with glad tongue Thy tender mercies own—
Except Thou pity, Christ, we are undone!

BOOK IV

THE BEGINNING OF THE HOLY WAR

XXXIV

In Galilee—Mission of the Twelve

Now, in all the cities Jesus went about
Teaching in synagogues; to poor, unlearned,
Preaching words of their life; did any ail,
He healed,—in village, city, open waste!
Multitudes, souls distressed, cried out on Him,
Revealed that hunger no man had supplied—
For word of God to strengthen. Scattered sheep,
That went unshepherded until Jesus came!

The Christ, perceiving how the people fed
On milk of the Word like babe at mother's breast,
Went out to them as mother to her young
In wistful pity, would upgather these,
His babes distressed and scattered, wanting milk!
The mother who hath sons, babes of her womb,
Distressed and scattered on a foreign shore
Where no man pities, gives them bread to eat,
Some measure hath she of the heart of Christ
Beholding how His children go unfed,
Unguided in a land where, for His sake,
None comforts them with love nor feeds with grace!
Ah, Christ, give us compassion, that we go
To teach Thy scattered folk the thing we know!

Were those at hand the Lord would send with bread
Hither and thither where the hungry be:
Nay, they themselves with a harvest ripe to cut,
Plenteous and bountiful—that multitude
Hung famished on His word! Then turned He round
To His disciples: Have ye understood
How all the poor stand ready to your hand,

A golden harvest to be gathered in?
Say ye, they know not letters, have small need
Of that which feeds man's spirit? Nay, I say,
Each hath been sown of God, and reared, and waits
That word shall as a sickle cut his heart
And lay him ready to be garnered in
To th' Kingdom he was made for. Pray ye, then,
The Lord of the harvest labourers to send
East, West, and North and South, lest this good grain
For want of harvesting rot on the ground:
Plenteous the harvest, but the labourers few!

Then called He forth the Twelve, the Chosen Men,
Should speed His message to remotest shore:
And two by two He sent them, lest their heart
Should fail them in an alien world alone.
With rich endowment sent He these abroad—
Graced with authority, His proper part,
To cast out devils, all diseased to heal,
And preach to men, The Kingdom of God is come!
The message still is ours to spread abroad:
Creative Energy, His attribute,
But lent He for those early days of the Church,
The Bridegroom yet at hand, or scarce withdrawn!
We know the Twelve, can name the blessed names
Of them went with the Lord, the Gospel learnt
At the very lips of Christ: thus charged He them:—

XXXV

Charge to the Twelve

"Go not in way of the Gentiles; nor so much
As enter city of Samaria;
To Israel your message; speak it there
Where be the chosen people."

("But, why, dear Lord The very words of life,
Be they not for us all?" Yea, but, perchance,
The Sower sows where soil is full prepared,
And God had not made ready.)

"To My lost sheep of Israel shall ye go—
Unshepherded of any, for their lords
Do take at will the good things of the Word
Nor feed the sheep, anhunger'd.

"Poor sheep, tell them, the Kingdom is at hand
Where God doth rule, His people feed and play,
And gather duteous at their Father's feet
Whilst He discourseth music.

"And find ye hindrance, be there many sick,
Lepers unclean and poor souls devil-bound,
Nay, be there very dead,—be not constrained,
By any evil hindered.

"Behold, I give you of My potency,—
That which is God's—Authority to deal
With every evil doth oppress man's state:
Then, freely give ye likewise.

"Rich go ye in My gift and carry wealth
For healing of the nations: take ye not
The wealth of men, or gold or brass in purse;
No virtues be in these things.

"No, not so much as wallet shall ye take
To hold the alms of th' faithful: nor take shoes
To ease the heavy ways, nor second coat
Nor staff, nor crust for your need:

"Am I not with you all the way ye go?
Doth any Lord send famished servants forth
To do his bidding? Am I less than these?
Assured my servant's bread, then.

"For, worthy he who laboureth for Me.
And each householder shall My Almoner be
His table to provide, his needs supply—
Who faithful bears My message.

"That roof is honoured which doth shelter you,
So find out who is worthy ere ye lodge;
Then enter and abide the while ye stay
In that same city, village.

"Enter that house with reverent salute,
Nor cross ye arrogant the man's threshold;
And, lo, your peace shall as a river flow
In that house, be it worthy!

"Unworthy is the house, its inmates all
Given o'er to lust of flesh and lust of eye!
Though ample meats they offer, go ye thence—
Your peace departing with you.

"Go ye to village where no man will hear,
Where chaffering and feasting all their care,
Nor have they leisure for one thought of Me!—
Leave ye that house, that city:

"But, for they have defiance cast at God,
Rejecting you whom I sent for their help,
The very dust shake off your feet in sign
God also them rejecteth.

"One speaks word, and he who hears it goes
Or thinks upon it or light lets it pass;
What matter, saith he, for a spoken word,
Is a man bound by sayings?

"But, I tell you, man's most chief concern
Is not with work and circumstance of life;
'Tis by the words he hears a man is judged,
And how he doth receive them.

"Therefore, no virtues, sins, cross accidents,
No prospering or failure can at all
Compare with words ye speak to damn a man
In judgment, or to save him.

"And whatso town refuse to take you in
Or hear the priceless words ye bring to them,
They have condemned themselves; Gomorrah's sin
And Sodom's less than theirs is."

Ah, Lord, make us to know what things import,
And how the word received by us is more
Than any wealth or loss; that we be judged
By that we hear and hold by!

And, Lord, make us regard our city's ways,
Labour that all the folk discern the truth,
Nor toil for spurious values, tinsel shows,
But know, Thy Word—their treasure!

XXXVI

The Charge—Of Dangers

I SEND you forth, My friends, as simple sheep,
    With ruthless wolves about;
Harmless as doves in all your goings keep,
    The serpent's guile without;
But see ye learn his wisdom; quick to see
    When danger comes your way;
Hunt they, wide-mouthed, upon you? turn and flee,
    Nor fall, a heedless prey;
For, more than your own life guard ye with wile,
    My Word is in your hand:
See that ye guide your ways with innocent guile,
    And keep ye in the land!

Beware of men, I say; alert are they,
    On every hand they wait;
That they may learn? Nay, watching night and day,
    Then are they most elate
When unconsidered words put in their power
    The lives of simple men,
My servants; before Council in that hour
    They bring you; and again;
In synagogue they scourge you; stripes two score
    Save one, on you are laid;
Their Kings and governors arraigned before, —
    Your testimony's made!

Nor take ye heed how ye that witness bear,
    Nor anxiously forecast;
The Spirit shall Himself be with you there,
    'Tis He shall speak at last!
And ye, content, perceive that words have come

      Beyond your power to think:
"Now, gladly would we be thus ever dumb,"
      Ye cry, as low ye sink
And praise your God who hath deliverance brought
      In that so perilous hour;
The Spirit of your Father, He hath wrought
      Wisdom in you, and power!

But, ah, my children, hate shall hem you round,
      And all for My name's sake;
Brother, his brother shall deliver bound
      To them his life will take:
Nay, father with his own child by the neck
      Shall come before the judge,
Witness shall bear against him, nor shall reck,
      Nor blood of offspring grudge!
Now, what strange sight is this? A son draws near,
      His mother in his hand;
He tells, how she the Christ doth reckon dear,
      So brings her by command!

The blood of her who bore him sees he fall,
      Nor groans aloud nor weeps;
Madness of hatred doth his soul enthral
      And him from pity keeps!
See ye, no easy service have ye ta'en,
      Who under Me would serve;
But, come ye to extremity of pain,
      E'en then will I preserve!
Wise in your generation shall ye be;
      When persecutions rise,
Into another city take and flee,—
      For, long serves he who flies.
Ah, Lord, was ever won by Chief
With words presaging loss, disaster, grief!

XXXVII

The Charge—Of Fears

WOULD ye then go at ease, your Lord oppressed?
Nay, be ye as your Lord,—rejected, poor,
From no rude insult shielded: have they not
Confounded Christ with devils, deeds benign,—
Blasphemous, to Beelzebub ascribed?
Shall ye fare better than your Master? Go
Observed and honoured where your Lord's condemned?
My service great estate conferreth not
On him waits My commands; go, seek ye then
Another service for a prouder pay
If Mine content you not.
                      But have no fear,
Electing, ye, to stay with Me and serve!
Their ways are known of God, their secret thoughts,
And private things men whisper and conceal,
Plots laid with craft, false witness cunning-taught,
And guileless men these compass to destroy —
All these shall show in the light and men shall see:
When God himself is judge, why should ye fear?
Lo, what in darkness speak I, in dead hour
Of silent night drop in your wakeful ear,
That word ye shall make known, shall cry aloud
Insistent, cry from the housetops, nothing feared
For missiles and hard words against you hurled.

My friends, there is but one whom ye shall fear;
Not them who kill the body—what of that,
Killed for My sake, alive forevermore!
There is, who worse death works—through fear or sloth,
Or selfish love of ease or greed of gain,
Bids men eschew My service—fear ye him

Who knows to kill men's souls; none other fear!
But ye, why should ye fear? See ye yon small birds,
Two sparrows for a farthing, poor men's meat!
The birds are dear to God; not one shall fall
But He takes notice: are ye less than they?
Weary you not with thought of all the world
Hanging dependent on the Father's care,
And ye—so small, what mattereth your fate?

But understand, each one hath place with God
As stood he single in the universe!
How shall one make you know the Father's care,
How intimate, how tender! Consider, ye,—
The very hairs of your head be numbered all.—
The finger-scratch, small ache that vexes you,
The garments of your choice, all little things—
Are noted, fatherly, by Him who made,
Sustains and wise-chastiseth. Fear ye not!

Ye men who hear My word, to you hath God
Given chance of great obedience; go, confess
The Lord ye serve before men—remembering
The day shall come when all men, gathered, wait
The judgment of the Father: then will I
Go, take him by the hand who Me confessed,
And straight before My Father in high heaven—
"This man is My own friend," shall I declare:—
He that denies shall that day be denied.

Think not the Prince of Peace sends peace on earth;
A sword shall go before Me, sets at twain
A daughter and her mother, father and son,
Till they of a man's household be his foes!
The son shall love the Christ, the father, hate;
And he that hateth, run to testify,—
"See, this, my son, a follower of false gods,

Of Him they call Messias! I bring him you!
The Law, look you, is more than flesh and blood,—
So take my son; nay, kill him an ye will!"
None shall be safe; relations peep and pry;
Who speaks with whom, they note, and catch stray words;
"Lo, she is of that sect, and he, and he!"
They cry to Council, delivering them to death.
Mother will plead that day—"For my sake, son,
Give up strange doctrines and obey the Law!"
But, whoso loveth mother more than Me,
Father or son or daughter,—for their sake
Wills to deny his Lord,—that man, I say,
Is not found worthy of Me. Other loves
A man shall hold in My Love; none prefer!
What father keeps his cherished son from risks
Attending his King's service? Am I less,
That ye should slight and set My name aside
When perils threaten? Say ye, "Life is sore
When one's against a household, when all vex,
Incessant argue, plead and press their cause;—
Might but a man keep silence, all were well!"
But, I say, he that loveth kith and kin,
Father or child, or his own easy life,
More than he loves his Master, unworthy, he,
To get that Pearl of price, that Sum of life—
Christ, who will give HIMSELF to him who loves
As bridegroom gives to bride—reserving nought!

XXXVIII

The Cross—The Master

My children, see, before you as ye go,
    A shape of dread;
Close as your shadow, ever lying low
    On path ye tread—
See its two arms extended, straight mid-line—
    Ye know the sign!
Image of shame, it is the Cross ye see,
Cross raised for Malefactors—and for Me!

And ye who follow shall take up your cross,
    Nor fear the shame;
Shall suffer gladly ignominy, loss,
    Good neighbor's blame:
To stand ye well with men, seek not at all,
    But give Me all!
The thing ye shrink from, hate, that go and do,—
Lo, I am with you alway, the day through!

None followeth Me but lifts and bears that weight
    Through slights and scorn,
Through trials manifold, through anguish great,
    Despised, forlorn!
Disciple, he who bears the bitter cross
    To this world's loss:
See, he is worthy of that fullest bliss,—
Reserved for him who loves—The Bridegroom's kiss!

But he who finds his life, its grace and joy,
    Men's praise, success,
Who spends his easy days without annoy
    He shall go less!
The life he chooseth shall elude his grasp;

        His fingers' clasp
Shall not retain those joys he held so dear;
ME he hath bartered for things small and near!

But who for My sake his dear life shall lose—
        Each fond delight,
Each pleasure perilous shall straight refuse
        In My sole might,—
I tell you, that he gives, he finds again;
        And every pain
Sustained for Me becomes a jewel, wrought
In that fair crown for him on Cross I bought!

XXXIX

A PASSING CROSS—THE DISCIPLE

MY soul, and whence is this to thee!
Would'st know if so great marvel be,
That Jesus Christ should condescend
To dwell, thy close, abiding friend?

Ask not alone of gracious moods,
When peace with wings of healing broods,
And meekness, love, and patience sit,
Disciples, at those wounded feet.

If Christ doth truly dwell in thee,
Uneasy Inmate will He be;
A heavy Presence, sighing, sad,
Shall oft defy thee to make glad

With any joy that sense can bring;
In vain thou stirr'st thy heart to sing
As though no care oppresse'd thy state;
A Man of Sorrows, He doth wait

Till thou be moved to hear His plaint;
Till thou perceive it is thy taint,
The plague spot of an alien heart,
That moves Him to so sad a part!

And then—ah, when, His grief made thine,
When penitence, sharp grace divine,
Doth the corrupting spot atone
In tears, all His, and yet thine own,—

Thy springing heart, a child's again,
Forgetting all the former pain,
Is jocund with the temper'd mirth
Of souls new wash'd to their new birth!

XL

A SECRET CROSS—THE DISCIPLE

A FATHER, who his sons would send
To goal remote for weighty end,
First called, and bound on each the load
Whose conduct safe upon the road
Was their chief care; on each that share
His strength just fitted him to bear.
At first scarce noting that they bore,
Anon the burden presses sore
Upon the weaker of the two.
The father, wise, had out of view
Bound on their backs the load; now he
Doth bring it round, its bulk to see;
Then in his hands doth poise, and sigh,
And to his comrade dol'rous cry,—
"My brother, do but feel the weight!
How walk, sustaining such a freight?
Nay, rather, let me ease on thee
But one end of my load, so we
May go with equal pace!" Agreed,
But ever tardier proves their speed:

Uneven steps, ill-balanced weight,
Doubles for each his former freight.—
"Good brother, couldst thou bear the whole?
I know thee strong, a valiant soul,
And I so weak! full sweet it were
Thus onward in thy strength to fare!"
Forgetting that he bears behind,
The brother yields, ere long to find,
A wisdom surer than his own
Had given a burden which, alone,

Was all his strength could well sustain:—
"Nay, thou must take thy load again,
It is too much; and why shouldst thou
Go free, while I twice-burden'd bow?"
Whereat his brother plains and frets,
But still to take his load forgets:—
"I thought thou lov'dst me; now I know
Thy fondness but a treacherous show!"—
Thus, hearts divided, thenceforth, they
Fall out and strive upon the way.

All other burdens men may share,
And brother, kind, for brother bear;
'Neath Self, each soul must go alone!—
Nor for this isolation moan,
Nor pity thee that none may know
Thy craving Self's peculiar woe:
Nor sympathy, exacting, crave
For every mood or gay or grave;
Nor entertain thy brother's ear
With all thy hope and all thy fear;
Nor tell each trifling discontent
Another's heedless ways have lent;
Nor thy more intimate concern—
How love grows cold, how love doth burn,
Nor how thy prayer doth not prevail—
Make not of secret grief thy tale:
Bear it, an unregarded weight,
With forward step, eye steadfast, straight,
And, lo, forgot, it disappears,
The burden that oppress'd thy years!
Another, tenderer yoke is laid,
Whose heaviness is all o'erpaid
By the sweet sense of service given;
Bearing, thou mov'st to-day in heaven!

XLI

The Cross—The Disciple

Fairer than all the sons of men,
Lovely beyond high seraph's ken,
The beauty of the Lord our God upon Him—
O wherefore say'st thou we should not desire Him?

A sacrifice, with red wounds scarr'd;
Ah, pity He should be so marr'd;
But dear love tokens are these stripes upon Him,
And more than any grace do bind us to Him.

. . . . .

Fast bound, a living sacrifice,
With silent lips and patient eyes,
And outspread hands that grasp not any treasure,
And nailed feet that move not on His pleasure:—

Looking, our hearts do sink in fear;
Seen from afar, how fair! Drawn near,
The vision of the Lamb appalls! Sore paineth
Us, this continual Dying that constraineth!

XLII

The Charge—Of Receiving a Disciple

Who opes a door of welcome wide
And prays that ye with him abide,
Who spreads his best to entertain,
Tho' all his best be poor and plain—
That man another guest receives;
Behold, his King doth come that day
With the poor, humble man to stay!
Nay, God Himself doth condescend
To visit that man as His Friend:

A good man's friends have many friends;
All do him grace a prophet sends;
Shall My disciples not ensure
Much good for them, their good procure?
Doth it not count, a man should grace
Servants I send before My face?
I tell you, yea; no gift beguiled—
Cup of cold water to a child—
From any man by word ye speak
But its reward from Me shall seek:
Who honours you, he serveth Me;
Safe stands he in his lot, and see,—
His undertakings all are blest,
Misfortunes do not him molest:
Not that man's debtor will I be
Who serves the friend who serveth Me!

XLIII

The Mission—On the Way

The men went forth wherever highways led:
In open ways these went as did their Lord,
For by the wayside all the cities sate;
And hidden villages by winding paths
Joined them, too, to the channel carried life,
The road all sorts of people went upon;—
The village folk, the daintier men of towns,
Scribes, Pharisees and publicans, grave priests,
And they who tilled the land; rude wagons drawn
By patient large-eyed oxen, slow of pace.
The man who stands and ponders, imaged sees—
In the thick-peopled plains, the cities fair,
The traffic of the road,—all the wide world
Enacting all its ways.
                    These two who pass,
With speech incessant, gesticulation free,
Too rapt are they t' observe those roadside sights
Had otherwise amused them mightily:
And all the wayfarers, concerned were they
Each with his own affairs, nor took much heed
Of what spake they, the Two, walked without staff
Or script, or aught the common traveller bears
To ease him on his way. Afire, their hearts,
With words of life they carried from the Christ!
Trembled they for the thought of prisons, stripes,
All perils them awaited? "Freely give,
For freely have ye gotten," was His word;
And burned their hearts as they told o'er the coins
Of priceless truth they carried—mighty freight!
Which first to spend—that simple tale of Sower,
Or Christ's word of the New Law and the Old,

Or tale of some great sign their eyes had seen?
As purse compact so full no single coin
Can we dislodge but all come pouring forth,
E'en so these men, who such full treasure held,
Scarce could they pick out small coin for the way!
"Let's take the path to yonder village; lo,
That word most fit shall come to us at need!"

XLIV

The Mission—The First Two

THEY reached the village; lifted voice
To arrest the passers: bade, "Rejoice,
The King is come, Messias all men wait;
Come, press ye through the Kingdom's narrow gate!"
Men gave a passing glance—scarce lent an ear;—
What was't to them Messias should appear?
Busy were they with great concerns;
"Who has to till the soil, he learns,"
Say they, "that every idle tale
Must not to stop men's work prevail."
This one and that had each bought field;
Inquired, anxious, of its yield,
And whether millet, corn or vine
Were best for first crop to assign:
"Poor dreamers, these, now what know they
How men must toil all through the day
Shelter to keep above their head
And get their little children, bread?"
Said labouring men, and turned away,
Nor would mere words to hear delay.
This friendly man said, "Come and sup,"—
But would not take their doctrine up,
Nor for an instant lend a listening ear
To all they would unfold of hope or fear!

Sad, they went forth from village street,
And shook the dust from off their feet!

XLV

THE MISSION—THE SECOND TWO

THESE other TWO to city came;
In crowded streets they would proclaim
Him, came the multitude to teach;
Here, like their Master, would they preach:
A haughty scribe gibed and passed by;
Priest, arrogant, aloud did cry,—
"These ignorant, why come they here
Us to instruct, and have no fear?"
The people heard the scornful word
Their rulers speak: lightly deterred,
They quit the men whose words had seemed
Touched with a glory they had dreamed.
Alone, rejected, stood the TWO,
But yet their mission would pursue: —
"In yonder street, perchance, there be
Men less averse to Christ; go we
And tell them of that gracious Lord
Who bade us hither with His Word."
They spake, but no man stopped to hear;
Full of diverse concerns appear
The poor and rich alike; what heed
Give they to tales of "lamp" and "seed,"—
Such themes were as an idle song,
Powerless to stay that busy throng!
They, sorrowful, departing, must
Shake from their shoes that city's dust.

XLVI

The Mission—The Third Two

A BLIND man at the city gate
Begged alms begrudged,—ah, wretched fate!
The TWO just stood and gazed;
Soon gathered there a crowd, amazed
That any should regard the sight
Of man, deprived of heaven's light!
The TWO conceived the poor man's state,
And understanding, pity, great,
Melted their hearts: they spake His Name
To witness of whose grace they came:—
"In name of Jesus, ope thine eyes!"
The folk await what comes; surprise
And mocking insolence contend
In every mind, —"Why, here's a friend
Worth having, if His name suffice
To open blind eyes in a trice!"
But, see, the blind man first looks around—
Gone mad with sight, leaps from the ground!
A radiant joy his face illumes,
Air of a free man he assumes,
He sees and looks and looks and sees
Men's faces, branches in the breeze;
The blessed sun, all life's sweet shows;—
Then, grateful, falls at the feet of those
Conferred inestimable boon
And made him see! The people soon
Pressed close; recovered of amaze,
Fixed on the TWO their ardent gaze,
And listened long and learned well,
What those Apostles had to tell.
"Nay, leave us not thus soon," they cried,

"Within our city's walls abide
Till many hear the wondrous news
Ye bring of Him, the Christ." "Refuse
Not shelter of a poor man's roof!"
Cried one till then had stood aloof:
They went with him and there remained
For many days, and still explained
Such mysteries of the Kingdom as they knew;
And many sick they healed and great signs did
    they do.

XLVII

THE MISSION—THE FOURTH TWO

"YOU'RE welcome to my house, good friends,
But who his proper business tends,
He can't give heed to doctrine strange,—
Matters so far beyond his range
He could not comprehend, not he,
Thought he of nothing else! For me,
I leave such questions to the priests,
While I lay fodder for the beasts
That well repay my kindly care:
I go e'en now to see how fare
Five yoke of oxen I have bought;
Sufficient for my time and thought
To prove how these will go in plough;
Small time for dreaming farmer hath, I trow!"
So spake that man, nor gave the Apostles leave
To show him of these things he should believe:
The day's work all his care, he went his way:
The TWO had come to him might not delay
In village prosperous where that man dwelt,
Where all men's thoughts with crops and cattle dealt:
What need had they of more? The TWO depart,
Dust shaken from their feet, with sorry heart.

XLVIII

The Mission—The Fifth Two

"Nay, foolish fellow, I have wed a wife!
Know what that means and ye may talk of life!
What's this of Kingdom, pearls, a Lord t' obey?
The word shall rule me, my own wife doth say!
'Tis but a few days since I made her mine;
Scarce have I watched her eyes grow soft and
    shine,—
And ye would have me turn my thoughts away
From her, delight of days! Why, e'en the Law
Allows a man a year ere it would draw
Him from his new-made wife for any cause;
Are ye, poor dreamers, greater than our laws?
Ye talk of faith and joy and that vast prize
He takes who lays up treasure in the skies:—
'Tis here and now that I my treasure taste;
There's nought but love; and he whose hope is based
On love of wife or child or tender friend,
Their fond embraces, of his days, the end;—
Why that man takes and eats, as he goes on,
Of fullest joy man knows beneath the sun!"
So prated he, and sealed th' Apostles' lips;
For who in fleshly slough his senses dips,
His thought is drowned: of Christ, what need
    hath he,
In sensual transports, all whose raptures be?

XLIX

Love's ordering: A paraphrase—Disciple

Say'st, "love is sweet," young heart,
    "A natural law, and light?"
Thou know'st not love: thy poorer part,
    The sensible delight
Affection stirs in nerves and blood,—
So fond, so fervent, now;—and now, averted, rude.

Holy is love; hedged round
    With fiery "shalt not:" hear
What disabilities do bound
    True love; lest it appear,
Condemned in that thou dost allow,
Thou, willing what love ought, to do discern not how.

In word shalt thou not love:
    Ah me, all dulcet dreams
And "tender morning visions!" when to prove
    Himself the god he seems,
Thy love lifts gates that shut him in
From emprises Olympian, sweet awards to win!

Plainest, "hard the measure,
    Ungenial is the law,
That would ban life's tend'rest pleasure! —"
    Nay, then, didst never draw
On dreams of service to reprove
Return thou thought'st too measur'd for unordered love?

Nor shall thy facile tongue
    Love's sacred substance spend
On the sweet tale too frequent sung.—

Thou question'st, "to what end?"
Alas, young heart, vows seal the eyes!
What if thou miss some altar, set for sacrifice?

Wouldst know the worth and meed
    Of love thou crav'st to speak?
Appraise alone by duteous deed,
    Or by refrainings meek.
One further doubt;—dost lay out love
With narrow merchant thought, return in kind to move?

Nay, but love thou in truth,
    And not for any hope,
But fervently, in loyal sooth:
    Though deed should win no scope,
Yet hath he love's divinest part
Who truly bears another in his steadfast heart!

L

The mission—The sixth Two

INTO poor city came the other TWO
Where was disease and famine: "Let us do
What may be for these men; speak words of peace
Shall instant bring the suffering soul release
From intolerable bonds of his distress:—
'Friends, suffering friends, we bring but words to
    bless,
But, pray you, hear of Him, has come to reign,
Men to release from hunger, sin and pain!' "
They told in tender words how Christ for men
Full forty days had fasted; hungered, then,
Satan solicited with every wile
He useth fainting outcast to beguile;
And how, for men's sake, He repelled attack—
That never sufferer, anhungered, lack.
"Words, idle words," a hardened fellow cries;
"Where is the man with words his meat supplies?"
But all the people knew them fed and eased
By thought of Him who graciously was pleased
To suffer hunger, every poor man's pain,
That famished men to fulness might attain.
"Nay, share our scanty meat, with us abide,
Your words be bread to us!" the people cried:
And there through those distressful days they stayed,
And ministered with healing; preached and prayed.

LI

THE DEATH OF JOHN THE BAPTIST

SEE, in grim fastness by Dead Sea,
Unwonted signs of revelry!

Soldiers and servitors about,
Bold chafferers with noisy rout;

Gay cavalcade and grave, great lord,
To council called, or festive board; —

By all these signs, the King, we know,
Come with his ladies, lords enow:

The desert he makes populous
With all his train tumultuous!

. . . . .

See, Herod sits in state amongst his lords,
Who watch his eye, acclaim his vainest words:

The wine flows free; the king has liberal grown,
No churl is he to-day, but spends his own:

Who enters there? A maiden rare to see,
Intruder on the royal revelry:

. . . . .

Now see her dance, give play to all her grace,
Till sensuous rapture shines on every face:

Salome, daughter of a mother wise,
Displays her graces in the monarch's eyes.—

A draught for every lip at royal board;
The King is grateful, nay, he will accord

Gifts fair, most rich! Now see him in his wine
Rise, liberal, to give: "It shall be thine,

If half my kingdom serve thee! Have no fear;
The boon thou cravest shall not prove too dear,

Too hard for him, the King, thou grac'st to-day
With thy fair beauties' generous display!"

"My opportunity!" Salome thought;—
"Now, what to choose? estates, or slaves, or gold?"

Bewildered, all embarrassed by too much
Almost in grasp,—"I'll to my mother go!
This moment is too golden for my use;
The Queen will better know to name that gift
The king in his cups would grace me with to-day!"
Her mother sought she, (who had decked her out,
Foreseen the issue, waited eager, strain'd,
To learn,—the king did generous incline
To give the utmost Salome should beg):
"What shall I ask, my mother?" Never doubt
She had her answer ready: "What to thee
The King's most lavish gift—to half his realm?
Hath the King aught that is not mine and thine?
How shall he give thee what e'en now thou hast?
We lift full cup—but poison's in the draught;—
My life's abhorred for John Baptist's sake!
Would I were dead, unknowing how the King
Lends ear to John; grave, ponders all his prate,

And tells me, me! how sore his conscience works,
For John hath bid him put away his wife
Due-mated to another! Herod is weak!
Why heeds he all this talk of righteousness,
Of tempered rule of flesh,—judgment to come,—
That day by day to hear he seeks out John,
Unkingly, in his dungeon? leaves my side
In hour of dalliance sweet; at public joust
Allows me to sit alone while steals he forth
To sit at feet of his prophet—so he styles
This bedouin of the desert!—trembles to hear,
(And tells me how he trembles!) this rude man
Denounce to his face the King, his nobles great,
The careless ways of th' court, and chief of all,
The Queen he hates—knowing the easy king
Would yield him to his guidance, I, removed!
Now, mark me, girl! A day will come, and soon,
Your mother's blood shall wash away that sin
John tells him he hath done in wedding me!
No rest, no joy have I, nor sleep nor play
Yields me an interval from thought,—
How I shall compass his, my enemy's, life!
He, dead, full easy sit I on the throne
With none to share dominion o'er the king—
His public acts and his most secret thoughts!
But, John alive, tasteless as Dead Sea fruit
Those envied honours, riches, reverence, joys,
Fall to my share as Queen!

                "And yet thou ask'st,
Callous of heart as young things wont to be,
'What boon, my Mother, ask I of the King?'
Return to th' feast, cry out before his lords,—
'Give me John Baptist's head!' Herod, ashamed
To break his silly word 'fore all his court,

Will straight commission one to go with axe,
Cut head from his body—would that I were there!—
No puling, now,—in the King's presence wait
Till he come back—red axe, and bleeding head
Borne stately on a charger; steady thy heart;
Lift thou with thine own hands the ghastly dish,—
Bring hither to thy Mother! She will bless
(If any God hear prayer of blood-stained lips!)
The daughter who by one consummate act
Shall ease her Mother's life of every grief!"
Salome heard, infected by the rage
Of love and jealousy, wild headlong hate,
Her mother's words imparted: forth she went, —
In strength of borrowed passion, begged her boon:
And he, the greatest born of woman, fell,
Slain by a woman's hate of righteousness!

LII

JOHN THE BAPTIST

NO great man lives in vain; the tale is told
A hundred ages after, how he, bold,
Went forth to meet the dragon, slew the beast,
While the delivered kingdom, glad, increased
In wealth and peace and happy progeny,
And blessed their saviour—sure, a great one, he!
Some, great, with poet-words go forth to bless,
And some, with mighty deeds of righteousness;
Some, fruit of knowledge snatch from branches high
Of sacred Tree few men are bold to try.
What then did John that we should know him great,—
Aware he hath enriched each man's estate
Of them that have come after? What owe we
To the Great Baptist? Thankful, would we be!

Image of dread, axe laid to root of tree,
Threatens our hours of wilful levity;
That life in desert spent, devoid of ease,
Chides us at moments we the flesh would please;
That ringing cry, "Repent, God is at hand!"
Hear we when in the ways of sin we stand:
And, ah, the grace that cries to men, "Behold
The Lamb of God!" when hearts are proud and cold
As flesh of the dead, and all because of sin!

Sure, a great thing, by steadfast thought to win
A single nature-secret for men's use;
Or, thought, the world had hardly thought before,—
One guiding principle of life, from store
Eternal in the heavens, by which men live!
John's greatness 'twas, a few great thoughts to give

As bread to famished men; his flashing word
Is quick and powerful now as when first heard:
For evermore we know—Christ shall increase,
And we, in growing less shall find our peace:
We know,—a man receives not more or less
Than God bestows; the Good we take and bless
The Giver, grudging not 'gainst him hath more;
We know,—a man's fulfilled when but a Voice,
Emptied of all besides, he cries, Rejoice
For joy of Bridegroom's presence: know we, too
To discern Messiah tabernacled new
In this man, that man, even in me or you,
By sign of the Dove; meekness and love attest,
The King is present in that servant blest!
But these be fragments of great debt we owe
To him to whom 'twas given the Christ to know—
The very Lamb of God, should take away
The sins of all the world! take, day by day,
Till all that enmity men manifest
To God and to each other, at His hest,—
By alchemy divine He knows to use
On every heart doth not His act refuse,—
See, turn to pity, penitence and prayer,
And men confess, lo, Christ abideth there!
God, who dost deal his lot to every one,
We bless Thee, praise Thee, for Thy servant John!

LIII

Afterwards

NEWS reached those desert-men, John's followers,—
Their master, martyr to the truth, lay slain
In dungeon for the word,—"Not lawful is't
For thee thy brother's wife to take and wed."
Loud-echoing lamentations rent the air,
And cowed the King, sobered and full of fear
For that he'd done. Herodias—what of her
And Salome, who shared her mother's guilt?
Scourged by remorse, his whip, they live their days:
Ah, me, for the three guilty souls who heard
The long-drawn cries of them come there to mourn
Him, sent of God!
                    Bold, faced they Herod's wrath,
But found the King subdued and full of fear:
John's body come to beg, they took the corpse
And laid within a tomb—with wailing cries,
Issued from desolate hearts for aimless lives;
For what now should they do, their single work,
To do the Baptist's bidding, hear his word?
Where buried they the Baptist? Who can tell,
Or lonely in the desert by Dead Sea,
Or carried him away to city of the hills
Where lay his priestly fathers? Moses died,
And the Lord buried him—no man knew where;
God keepeth secret that may not be known
Lest good man fall on sin; the Baptist's grave,—
A place kept hid from men lest they should sin
In worship of that saint who died for truth?

Where in wide world these mourners should they go,
Grief desolated? They rose up and went

Day's journey two or three, where rumoured 'twas
The Christ was doing good. They told Him all.
We learn no more; but who hath sorrow faced,
Light of his life gone out, he knows the rest;
Knows there's no other place in all the world
For him to turn to, but where is the Lord;
Knows that a comforting which hath no words,
No touch, and scarce a thought, steals through his life;
Bound up, his broken heart, his heavy steps
Go lighter in the Way; he sees the dawn
Of hope in his dark heavens; goes renewed:
Might any 'bide our sometimes Comrade, Grief,
Save for that solacing at priestly hands
Of Him Who bare our sorrows?
Herod, meanwhile, confronted by the doubt—
May life go out? Tormented, for his friend
He'd slain with bloody hands for idle boast,—
Assured that John is somewhere, working works
And with those words of his searching men's souls
As strong winds search the forest; knowing well,
No final period comes to things like these,
No axe can shorten, nor grave cover up,—
This knowing, Herod heard in every blast
The Baptist's voice rebuking: saw in dreams
That rugged figure, emptied luxury
Of all enticement: nought might palliate
The King's uneasy pain, nor rest he knew
Nor any joy: "I am a Voice," said John,—
Said to him, Herod, "crying evermore;
In waste places of the wilderness, I cry!"
And in waste heart and arid of the King,—
"Why hast thou done this thing—who gave thee right
To take the life of prophet of the Lord?"

The breath of rumour ever brings new fears
To soul in torment: Herod heard of Christ,

His acts of healing and His words of grace:—
All men were full of talk of some new thing
Jesus had said—word never heard before;
Some sign he had wrought that sudden oped their eyes
Till God they saw at work, unveiled 'fore men!
Some said it was Elias come again;
Some, one of the old prophets; other some
Bethought them of the Baptist, said 'twas he:
Pallid with fear, the King heard every tale
And each man's guess, but spoke no word himself.
Troubled, perplexed was he, but not with doubt;
Full well assured the Baptist was alive,—
Death could not hold him—what did it portend,
To him, the murderer, had slain a man
Chosen of God and precious! Relief he sought
In reckless speech to his servants—"This is John
The Baptist, I beheaded. For judgment, lo,
He's risen from the dead! Would I might know
That he would have of me! Better to die
Than go in fear, accursed of men and God!"
Dreading and craving to see face of him
With bloody sword he'd slain, King Herod went,
A coward wretch; nor knew it was the Christ
Whose words and works were on the people's lips!

LIV

THE PASSOVER WAS NIGH

THE Passover was nigh; high Spring had come;
As when an army passing through a land
Leaves track of desolation, charred and sere,—
E'en so another host had passed that way
Leaving the land apulse with life and light!
Life had made her royal progress, hung her boughs
With rosy blossoms; made the waste to bloom—
Garden of flowers rich-painted, odorous;
Crept, greening through the grasses; flushed bare trees;
Set birds apairing, full of joy and song,
And brought all tender young things to the birth!
That marvel of the Spring had come to pass
And left the earth renewed; the dry and sere
Now burgeoned into life; the hoary earth
Was born again to gladness! Who can mark
The parable of the spring and take no heed,
Nor wonder at the upwards course the sap
Takes in the barren tree-trunk, finds its way
To furthest lateral branch and topmost twig,
And clothes bare limbs with miracle of leaves!
The little life laid up in gem-like egg,
Or that in bone-dry chrysalis, breaks forth;
And would men hold them from that fuss of days—
Affairs, so futile, fond, engross their thought—
Why, they might see *Life* early walk abroad
With movement, glow and beauty in her train;
Hear rhapsody and hymning in the air,
For what was dead hath come alive again!
But we are staled to wonders, slow of heart,
And greet surprises of the spring with eyes
Long used to things familiar—of small count!

The LORD of life, was't nought to Him to see
Through all things living, their green pulse renewed—
(Or red, or pale)—quickening the whole to life?
Took He no joy in multi-coloured veil
Spread sudden o'er the plains of Galilee,
Her mountain-slopes, her soft ethereal skies?
Sure, all the shows of earth were good to Him
As some great Minster to the architect;—
In such wise all things praise the hand that made!

A deeper joy was Christ's: the world of sense,
Astirring with new life, with beauty pranked,
Imaged for Him, how exquisite a life
Concealed in chrysalis dry as desert dust!
What sudden glory His foreseeing eye
Perceived break forth from this poor pilgrim, fraught
(And that), with dust of wayside, lying thick!
And His thoughts went out to the six great roads
Traversed all Galilee, north, south, east, west,
For flush of life discernible in crowds
Thronging the ways? perchance, to them, the Twelve,
As arteries, carried Life through all the plains,
The dry hard cities, thirsting villages!

LV

THE RETURN OF THE TWELVE

THE TWELVE come back, now two, now other two,
Till all had gathered there where was the Lord,
And each bare record in sweet countenance
Of that he had done, endured, seen come to pass,
While upon God's high errand. Each pair told
Of many villages and city crowds,
Of highways where they spoke to who would hear;
Of maimed and suffering to whom they brought
Christ's healing grace. Not one of them said, I
Spake this or that, did such a mighty work;
I and my fellow, we—was all their word.

Each pair had disappointments—told how men
Rejected them and that blest WORD they bare
As jewel in rough casket. How, the dust
Here, there and elsewhere they had shaken off
In testimony against men, refused to hear!
But, ah, of other things they told their Lord
With glistening eye, voice broken on the word!
How, here, whole city gave itself to God,
Brake into life, sudden as field in spring,
And clothed it in like beauty, fresh and sweet,
And goodlier growing as the days went on:
How, here, a stricken man, there, little child
Had seemed to see Messias eye to eye!
How, instant, hard dry souls converted, showed
The spring's assurance of new life and joy:
How men raised hallelujahs like the birds—
Gladness and singing greeted the new day!

Was't thus they spoke, and thus the Master heard,—
Gave grace of comprehension infinite,
Gladness of sympathy, ease of strong control?
And may fond fancy picture how each pair
Fared on that first great errand? Were it so,
Or otherwise, we know not; yet have we
Some license for thought reverent, for we, too,
Be sent on missions at the Master's word;—
We come with joyful tears or shame of heart
To tell how we have fared: is't well with us?
We know that HE has wrought through our weak words,
And bring Him of the first fruits. Is it ill?
How have we shamed the Master whose we are!

LVI

THE DESERT PLACE

THE LORD looked on the Twelve and saw their mood—
Tender of soul and sweet, but sore outworn
With all they'd done and felt these many days:—
"Come ye apart," saith He, "and rest awhile":
No leisure had they, not so much as to eat,
For ever-changing crowd hung round the Lord,
Some hung'ring for His word, others agape
For some new wonder, fit to make a tale.
He took them, went before to waterside,
Disciples following: there took He boat
To desert place, Bethsada, opposite;
And while they crossed, the men had more to tell
Of this one, that one, had been born again,—
Come forth in tender beauty of new life;
Nay, all their days would they repeat the tale
Remembering some new thing at every telling.

They reached the desert place—and lo, 'twas clothed
With waving grasses, jewell'd with bright flowers!
Each looked on other—saw an image true
Of how those barren lives late had they seen
Sudden transformed to glow of blossoming life:
In silent awe, they mutely praised the Christ,
With eyes acclaimed Him Lord of all men's souls!

LVII

L'Envoi

Good Lord, instruct us while we pore
    Upon Thy *Kingdom's* lore!
We know,—the King can raise the dead;
That, multitudes He nourished
On such small store as scarce could feed
One hungry lad; we know, indeed,
How tempests but display His power—
If all help faileth, then His hour,
    When a man's need is sore!

We know,—Thy kingdom is a prize
    For him will energize:
A man must diligent seek to find,
Bring eager heart and zealous mind,
And potent faith that can receive
Hard sayings, mysteries, believe;
That done,—Thy kingdom spreads apace
In its own strength; hath filled the place
    When we lift up our eyes!

Lord, draw us in Thy Kingdom's net,
Nor let us Thy Good Words forget!

INDEX

OF SUBJECTS AND REFERENCES TO PASSAGES
IN THE HOLY SCRIPTURES ON WHICH EACH
OF THE POEMS IS FOUNDED.

BOOK I

OF TAKING THE KINGDOM

I
The centurion's servant healed   23
St. Luke 7:1-10
St. Matthew 7:5-13

II
"Increase our faith."—The disciple   28

III
The raising of the widow's son   30
St. Luke 7:11-17

IV
John Baptist a prisoner   33
St. Luke 3:19-20

V
The message of John   35
St. Luke 7:17-24
St. Matthew 2:2-6

VI
The Lord testifies of John   38
St. Luke 7:24-35
St. Matthew 2:6-19

VII
The disciple dreams that he seeks instruction   43

VIII
A woman anoints His feet   48
St. Luke 7:36-50

IX
Circuit in Galilee—Women minister   51

BOOK II

PARABLES OF THE KINGDOM

X
Parable of the sower   55
St. Mark 4:1-9
St. Matthew 8:1-9
St. Luke 8:4-8

XI
Of teaching by parables   58
St. Matthew 8:10-17
St. Mark 9:10-12
St. Luke 8:9, 10

XII
The "sower" explained—1. The wayside   62
St. Matthew 13:18
St. Mark 6:15
St. Luke 8:12

XIII
The stony ground   65
St. Matthew 13:20, 21
St. Mark 9:16, 17
St. Luke 8:13

XIV
The seed among thorns   67
St. Matthew 13:22
St. Mark 9:18, 19
St. Luke 8:14

XV
The seed in good ground   69
St. Matthew 13:23
St. Mark 9:20
St. Luke 8:15

XVI
Of the hidden lamp   71
St. Mark 4:21, 22
St. Luke 8:16, 17

XVII
Parable of the tares and the wheat   72
St. Matthew 13:24-30, 36-43

XVIII
Parable of the seed growing secretly   75
St. Mark 4:26-29

XIX
The seed growing secretly—the disciple   77

XX
The mustard seed   79
St. Matthew 13:31, 32
St. Mark 4:30-32

XXI
The hidden treasure   81
St. Matthew 13:44

XXII
The leaven   84
St. Matthew 13:33

XXIII
The pearl of great price   86
St. Matthew 13:45-46

XXIV
The net cast into the sea   89
St. Matthew 13:47-50

XXV
"Have ye understood?"   91
St. Matthew 13:51, 52

XXVI
His mother and His brethren   94
St. Matthew 12:46-50
St. Mark 3:31-35
St. Luke 8:19-21

XXVII
"The same is My mother"—the disciple   96

XXVIII
Rejected   98
St. Mark 6:1-6
St. Matthew 13:53-58

XXIX
He could do no mighty works there   101
St. Matthew 13:58
St. Mark 6:5, 6

BOOK III

ADMINISTRATION OF THE KINGDOM

XXX
He stilleth the storm   105
St. Mark 4:35-41
St. Luke 8:22-35
St. Matthew 8:18, 23-27

XXXI
The demoniac restored   112
St. Mark 5:1-20
St. Luke 8:26-39
St. Matthew 8:28-34

XXXII
The maiden raised—The woman healed   117
St. Mark 5:21-43
St. Luke 8:40-56
St. Matthew 9:18-26

XXXIII
Two blind men restored,
and the dumb made to speak   121
St. Matthew 9:27-34

XXIII
The pearl of great price   86
St. Matthew 13:45-46

XXIV
The net cast into the sea   89
St. Matthew 13:47-50

XXV
"Have ye understood?"   91
St. Matthew 13:51, 52

XXVI
His mother and His brethren   94
St. Matthew 12:46-50
St. Mark 3:31-35
St. Luke 8:19-21

XXVII
"The same is My mother"—the disciple   96

XXVIII
Rejected   98
St. Mark 6:1-6
St. Matthew 13:53-58

XXIX
He could do no mighty works there   101
St. Matthew 13:58
St. Mark 6:5, 6

BOOK III

ADMINISTRATION OF THE KINGDOM

XXX
He stilleth the storm   105
St. Mark 4:35-41
St. Luke 8:22-35
St. Matthew 8:18, 23-27

XXXI
The demoniac restored   112
St. Mark 5:1-20
St. Luke 8:26-39
St. Matthew 8:28-34

XXXII
The maiden raised—The woman healed   117
St. Mark 5:21-43
St. Luke 8:40-56
St. Matthew 9:18-26

XXXIII
Two blind men restored,
and the dumb made to speak   121
St. Matthew 9:27-34

BOOK IV

THE BEGINNING OF THE HOLY WAR

XXXIV
In Galilee—Mission of the Twelve   127
St. Matthew 9:35-38; 10:1-4
St. Mark 6:6, 7
St. Luke 9:1

XXXV
Charge to the Twelve   129
St. Matthew 10:5-15
St. Mark 6:8-11
St. Luke 9:2-5

XXXVI
The charge—Of dangers   133
St. Matthew 10:16-23
St. Mark 6

XXXVII
The charge—Of fears   135
St. Matthew 10:25-37

XXVIII
The Cross—the Master   138
St. Matthew 10:38, 39

XXXIX
A passing cross—The disciple   140

XL
A secret cross—The disciple   142

XLI
The Cross—The disciple   144
Isaiah 53:2

XLII
The charge—Of receiving a disciple   145
St. Matthew 10:40-42

XLIII
The mission—On the way   146
St. Mark 6:12, 13
St. Luke 9:6

XLIV
The mission—The first Two   148

XLV
The mission—The second Two   149

XLVI
The mission—The third Two   150

XLVII
The mission—The fourth Two   152

XLVIII
The mission—The fifth Two   153

XLIX
Love's ordering: a paraphrase—Disciple   154
John 3:18

XL
The mission—The sixth Two   156

LI
The death of John the Baptist   157
St. Mark 6:17-28
St. Matthew 14:3-11

LII
John the Baptist   161

LIII
Afterwards   163
St. Mark 6:14-20, 29
St. Matthew 14:1-5, 12
St. Luke 9:7-9

LIV
The Passover was nigh   166
St. John 6:4

LV
The return of the Twelve   168
St. Mark 6:30
St. Luke 9:10

LVI
The desert place   170
St. Mark 6:21, 32
St. Matthew 14:13
St. Luke 9:10
St. John 6:1

LVII
L'envoi   171

Made in the USA
Las Vegas, NV
18 August 2023

76222808R00105